ANTIGUA RESERVA

Producto chileno elaborado y envasado
por Viña Ochagavia.
Grado alcohólico 12. Contenido 700 cc.

VIÑA OCHAGAVIA

Fundada en 1851

VINOS EXPOSICIO

Los Misioneros

Vino Tipo Asoleado

Envasado en Origen por C. A. Vitivinicola de Talca Ltda.
Avda. San Miguel 2631 – Talca
REGIÓN DEL MAULE

Grado Minimo 11.7 ... Chileno Contenido 700

TABLE WINE
VINTAGE
WILDMAN

Don Gabriel

CABERNET SAUVIGNON

PERALILLO, COLCHAGUA

VINO FINO, PRODUCIDO Y EMBOTELL
EN ORIGEN POR VIÑA LOS VASCOS
12.5% ALCOHOL BY VOLUME, 75... ml
PRODUCT OF CHILE

CONCHA y TORO

SPECIAL RESERVE

Marqués de CasaConcha

100% CABERNET SAUVIGNON
MAIPO RED TABLE WINE
PUENTE ALTO VINEYARD

ESTATE BOTTLED
GRAN VINO

ESTATE BOTTLED
LONTUE CHILE

VIÑA SAN PEDRO

Gato Blanco
Lontue Mosell...

CONTENTS 750 ML

CHILEAN WHITE WINE

PRODUCED & BOTTLED BY VIÑA SAN PEDRO S.A. SANTIAGO CHI

URMENETA

Established 1854

CHILEAN
Sauvignon Blan...

LONTUE
CHILEAN WHITE TABLE WINE
VINTAGE 1981

CONTENTS
375 ML.
ALCOHOL
12%
BY VOLUME

PRODUCT OF CHILE
BOTTLED IN CHILE BY VIÑA SAN PEDRO S.A. SANTIAGO – CHILE
IMPORTED BY LOS ANDES IMPORT INC. WEST NEW YORK, NEW JER...

1985

LOS VASCOS

SAUVIGNON BLANC

COLCHAGUA

Vino Fino Producido y Embotellado en
Origen por Viña Los Vascos. Peralillo.
PRODUCE OF CHILE
Propietarios
Jorge Eyzaguirre · María I. Echenique

MIGUEL TORRES
CHILE

B. 127

Bellaterra
Sauvignon Blanc

WHITE DRY WINE

750 m

Santa Carolina
CABERNET SAUVIGNON

★

ESTRELLA DE ORO

GRAN VINO CHILENO DE EXPORTACION

Producido y embotellado en Chile por Viña Santa Carolina S.A.
Grado alcohólico 12° Gl.   Contenido neto 0,70 l

...A LINDERO

Riesling
nombre varietal

...n distinción y encanto, marcado profu...
...clásico y refinado aroma varietal.

Sírvase frío

...embotellado en origen por Viña Linder
Ortiz S.A. - teléfonos 61665 y 87256
...DEROS-MAIPO-CHILE   Grado alc

Pajarete de Elqui
Vino generoso

HUANCARA

Producido y embotellado en el valle de Elqui por Cooperativa Agrícola Pisquera Elqui Ltda. Cupel
Camino a Peralillo s/n - Vicuña. Contenido 700 cc. Grado Alcohólico 16.50 gr G.L.
Producto Chileno - IV Región - M.R.

VIÑA MAIPO

VINO BLANCO

Vino Chileno
...oducido y embotellado por Viña Maipo, Chile
contenido neto 0.75 l
grado alcoholico 12 Gl.

SANTA HELE...
CHILEAN WINE
Rosé

Produced and bottled by Viñe... de Chile... R.Y
Santiago Chile

375 M L   ALC. 12

IMPORTED
...

ESTATE BOTTLED

Monte Cañeten

1984

COLCHAGUA

SAUVIGNON BLANC

Grown, Produced and Bottled by
Viña Los Vascos, Peralillo, Chile.
Imported by Wines of the World, Inc.
New York, NY, U.S.A.

PRODUCT OF CHILE

Alcohol 12.4% by Volume · Contents 750ml.

EMBOTELLADO EN ORIGEN

Castillo de Molina

CABERNET SAUVIGNON
VINTAGE 1978

VIÑA SAN PEDRO

DESDE 1865

CONTENTS 750 ML. ALCOHOL 12% BY VOL

PRODUCED & BOTTL...

IMPORTED
OF

PRODUCC
20.000
BOTELLAS

Pisco capel

selección 30°

PRODUCIDO Y EMBOTELLADO EN EL VALLE DE ELQUI (VICUÑA) PROVINCIA DE ELQUI - CHILE
POR COOPERATIVA AGRICOLA PISQUERA ELQUI LTDA. CAMINO A PERALILLO SIN
CONTENIDO

CABERNET SAUVIGNON

Santa Emiliana

1982

CONCHA y TORO

Errazuriz Panquehue M.R.

CORTON
GRAN VINO M.R.

Vino Elaborado y Embotellado por Viña Errázuriz-Panquehue Ltda.
Panquehue San Felipe CHILE

FOUNDED IN 1880

Santa Rita
MAIPO VALLEY CHILE

1986

SAUVIGNON BLANC
ESTATE BOTTLED

EXPORT WINE PRODUCED AND BOTTLED BY VIÑA SANTA RITA LTDA
...% BY VOL. 12%

EXPOSICION M.R.

Piña Espumante

Vino Suave Gasificado. Envasado en Origen por C.A. Vitivinicola de Talca Ltda. Avda. San Miguel 2631 - Talca - Región del Maule
Grado mínimo 9º G.L. - Producto Chileno - Contenido 750 c.c.

VINOS EXPOSICION M.R.

Conde del Maule

Envasado en Origen por C. A. Vitivinicola de Talca Ltda.
Avda. San Miguel 2631 — Talca
REGION DEL MAULE
Grado Mínimo 11,7 G.L. Producto Chileno Contenido 700 c.c.

1982

LOS VASC

CABERNET SAUVI
Peralillo, Colchagu

Vino Fino Producido y En
en Origen por Viña Los
PRODUCT OF CH
Propietarios
Jorge Eyzaguirre   María I. Ec

Licores
Campana

CONTENIDO 750 c.c.   PRODUC
LA SERENA IV REGION   GRADO ALCO
ELABORADO POR COOP. AGRICOLA
PISQUERO DE ELQUI LTDA

DAMASC

izuriz Panqu

DOÑA LEONOR
ANTIGUA RESERVA

Vino Elaborado y Embotellado por Viña Errázuriz-P
Panquehue, San Felipe - CHILE

VIÑA MAII
Importado por Importaciones Colombia Ltda.
Registro Minsalud N.º L 000240

Chilean
Burgundy

Grado Alcohólico 12° GL
Contenido neto 0.70 L
PRODUCTO CHILENO

Produccido
Viña Maipo

Vino Chileno de Exportacion

ANTIGUA RESERVA

Producto chileno elaborado y envasado
por Viña Ochagavia.
Grado alcohólico 12. Contenido 700 cc.

VIÑA
OCHAGAVIA

Fundada en 1851

VINOS EXPOSICIO

Los Misioneros
Vino Tipo Asoleado

Envasado en Origen por C. A. Vitivinicola de Talca Ltda.
Avda. San Miguel 2631 – Talca
REGION DEL MAULE
Grado Mínimo 11.7 ° Chileno Contenido 700

TABLE WINE
VINTAGE

FREDERICK
WILDMAN
AND SONS
NEW YORK CITY

Don Gabriel

CABERNET SAUVIGNO

PERALILLO. COLCHAGUA.

VINO FINO, PRODUCIDO Y EMBOTELLA
EN ORIGEN POR VIÑA LOS VASCOS.
12.5% ALCOHOL BY VOLUME. 750 ml.
PRODUCT OF CHILE

CONCHA y TORO.

SPECIAL RESERVE
Marqués
de
CasaConcha

100% CABERNET SAUVIGNON
MAIPO RED TABLE WINE
PUENTE ALTO VINEYARD

ESTATE BOTTLED
GRAN VINO

ESTATE BOTTLED
LONTUE CHILE

VIÑA SAN PEDRO.

Gato Blanco
Lontue Mosell

CONTENTS 750 ML   CHILEAN WHITE WINE

PRODUCED & BOTTLED BY VIÑA SAN PEDRO S.A. SANTIAGO CHI

URMENETA

Established 1851
CHILEAN
Sauvignon Blanc
LONTUE
CHILEAN WHITE TABLE WINE
VINTAGE 1981

CONTENTS   ALCOHOL
375 ML.   12°/o
PRODUCT OF CHILE
BOTTLED IN CHILE BY VIÑA SAN PEDRO S.A. SANTIAGO — CHILE
IMPORTED BY LOS ANDES IMPORT INC. WEST NEW YORK, NEW JER.

1985

LOS VASCOS

SAUVIGNON BLANC
COLCHAGUA

Vino Fino Producido y Embotellado en
Origen por Viña Los Vascos. Peralillo.
PRODUCE OF CHILE
Propietarios
Jorge Eyzaguirre María I. Echenique

MIGUEL TORRES
CHILE
M.R.

Bellaterra
Sauvignon Blanc   750 m

B. 127

WHITE DRY WINE

Santa Carolina

CABERNET SAUVIGNON

ESTRELLA DE ORO
GRAN VINO CHILENO DE EXPORTACION
Producido y embotellado en Chile por Viña Santa Carolina S.A.
Grado alcohólico 12º Gl.   Contenido neto 0,70 l.

Dibujo inédito de Thomas Daskam

A LINDERO

Riesling
– nombre varietal –

n distinción y encanto, marcado profu
clásico y refinado aroma varietal.
Sírvase frío
mbotellado en origen por Viña Linder
tiz S.A. - teléfonos 61665 y 87256
DEROS-MAIPO-CHILE   Grado alc

Pajarete de Elqui
Vino generoso
HUANCARA

Producido y embotellado en el valle de Elqui por Cooperativa Agrícola Pisquera Elqui Ltda.- Capel.
Camino a Peralillo s/n - Vicuña. Contenido 700 cc. Grado Alcohólico 16,50 gr G.L.
Producto Chileno - IV Región - M.R.

VIÑA MAIPO

VINO BLANCO

Vino Chileno
oducido y embotellado por Viña Maipo. Chile
contenido neto 0.75 l
grado alcohólico 12ºGl.

SANTA HELE

CHILEAN WINE
Rosé

Produced and bottled by Vinos de Chile S
Santiago · Chile

375 M L   ALC. 11.5

800 W. G
SUITE 33

IMPORTED

Chilean Wines

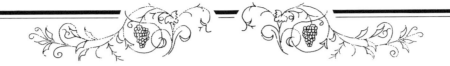

Chilean Wines

Jan Read

with an introduction and tasting notes by

Hugh Johnson

SOTHEBY'S PUBLICATIONS

First published 1988 for Sotheby's Publications
by Philip Wilson Publishers Ltd
26 Litchfield Street London WC2H 9NJ

Available to the USA Book Trade from
Sotheby's Publications
Harper & Row, Publishers, Inc
10 East 53rd Street New York NY 10022 USA

Exclusive distribution to the USA Wine Trade:
THE WINE APPRECIATION GUILD
155 Connecticut Street San Francisco California
94107 USA
(415) 566-3532

ISBN 0 85667 343 9
LCC 87-060746

Designed by Gwyn Lewis
Typeset and printed by BAS Printers Limited,
Over Wallop, Hampshire
Bound by Norton Bridge Bookbinders Ltd

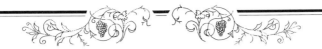

Contents

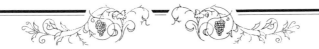

ODA AL VINO

Pablo Neruda

Vino color de día,	Wine the colour of day,
vino color de noche,	wine the colour of night,
vino con pies de púrpura	wine with purple 'legs'
o sangre de topacio,	or topaz blood,
vino,	wine,
estrellado hijo	starry son
de la tierra,	of the soil,
vino, liso	wine, smooth
como una espada de oro,	as a golden sword,
suave	suave
como un desordenado terciopelo,	as brushed velvet,
vino encaracolado	wine swirling
y suspendido,	and suspended,
amoroso,	loving,
marino,	of the sea,
nunca has cabido en una copa,	never bounded by a glass,
en un canto, en un hombre	a song or man,
coral, gregario eres,	choral, gregarious
y cuando menos mutuo.	or intimate and shared.

Acknowledgements

First, our thanks must go the Chilean Embassy in London and to its press attaché, Srta Olga Kliwadenko, who initiated the complicated arrangements for an extended visit to Chile. Our intricate programme within the country was arranged in consultation with the Chilean Traditional Wine Exporter Committee and with advice from Srta Monica Krassa Rowe of the Servicio Nacional de Turismo by the government export agency, ProChile. Our special thanks go to its then President, Don Ernesto Rendel, to Don Jorge Prieto and to Don Pablo Diaz, who so faithfully accompanied us on much of our journeyings. Our guides and mentors on visits to the Pisco area in the north and the cooperatives in the south were Don Rodrigo Jiménez of the Compañía Pisquera de Exportación Ltda and Don Emilio Merino Cisternas of the Federación Cooperativas Agrícolas Vitivinícolas, who, having treated us to an eloquent exposition of the wines for some 2,000 km, sped us on our way with a valedictory: 'I am, as you know, a man of few words.'

A host of wine-makers have helped in the preparation of the book by inviting us to their bodegas and laying on tastings of their wines. Among them, we should like to thank Don Alfonso Larraín Santa María, his brother Don Andrés, and Don Pablo and Don Eduardo Guilisasti of Viña Concha y Toro, with whom we spent a weekend at their estate in Peumo and who honoured us by the induction as members of the Gran Orden Casillero del Diablo. We were also the guests of Don Jorge Eyzaguirre and his wife Doña María Ignacia Echenique of Viña Los Vascos at their beautiful country house; but there cannot have been a winery in Chile which did not go out of its way to entertain and instruct us.

One remembers the elaborate press reception and charming *al fresco* lunch at Viña Santa Carolina; the tour of the historic old house and grounds at Viña Santa Rita; horse riding and a flight in a light aircraft at Viña San Pedro to survey the vineyards; the fairy-like beauty of the house and gardens at Viña Undurraga and the fascinating commentary of Don Pedro Undurraga on the origins of the Chilean wine industry; the country-style Chilean repast arranged by Don Eduardo Chadwick Claro of Viña Errázuriz Panquehue or, towards the end of the visit, the elegant reception in the house of Don José Rabat of Viña Manquehue – by which time, there was hardly an unknown face among our fellow guests from the wine community. The two major producers of pisco, the Cooperativa Agrícola Control Pisquera de Elqui Ltda and the Cooperativa Agrícola Pisquera de Elqui Ltda were equally helpful and hospitable.

As to the serious business of wine tasting, we were made welcome wherever we went, and notes of the tastings are printed in Chapter 7. One of the most useful of such exercises was the tutored tasting arranged by Don Fernando Ureta Cortes of the Facultad de Agronomía of the Universidad Católica in Santiago. We are grateful to all the many *bodegueros* whom space prevents us thanking individually.

The chapter on cooking was written with help from that doyen of Chilean gastronomes, Don Hernán Eyzaguirre Lyon, and we should also like to acknowledge the assistance of Doña Carmen Gandarillas of the Asociación Chilena de Gastronomía.

Like anyone who writes on Chilean wines, we are in debt to Don Rodrigo Alvarado Moore, who blazed the trail with his book *Chile tierra del vino*, the only existing study of the subject, and who was most generous with further information. Don Miguel A. Torres is an old friend, and as much an *aficionado* of Chilean wines as Spanish. Apart from a most interesting visit to his winery, where, in his absence, we were received by Don José Roca, his enthusiasm for the project encouraged us from the start.

Finally, most especial thanks must go to the wife of one of us (J.R.), Maite Manjón, who not only acted as interpreter throughout some 10,000 km of journeying, but has also contributed tasting notes and the chapter on Chilean cooking.

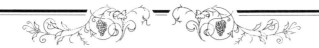

Introduction

The scene is a broad bungalow nine-tenths hidden by almost-tropical climbers and trees of great seniority. The sense of lush growth suggests the rainfall of Cork or Kerry: rivulets run and ferns fecundate in aromatic shades, cool despite a surprisingly high and direct sun. The verandah is on the grand colonial scale: a Long Gallery roofed but only one-walled, its peeling red-painted pillars supporting a broad barn roof of corrugated iron.

Dazzling white in the background, high above but improbably close, hangs the ridge of eternal snow that caps a mountain range so sudden that it seems to rise from the back garden to Himalayan heights.

Glowing deep red on the table before you is a glass of wine that seems both familiar and exotic. It bears a strong family resemblance to Bordeaux, and yet its flavour is round, ripe and open in a way that is rare in claret. It is very male wine, pungent and dry, dense in texture, hinting of resin, yet with a definite tannic cut that leaves your mouth fresh and ready for more.

The voices around you are speaking Spanish, but it is more leisurely, less clipped and emphatic than the Castilian sound.

You are in Chile. You are one of the elect who has gone beyond the mountains to a country of legendary fertility, which since the time of the Incas has been a cross between an allotment and the garden of Eden, a land that bestows its own romance on the traveller; that so stocks him with superlatives that he becomes a welcome story-teller on his return.

My introduction to Chilean wine was via a bottle that I mistook for a good Bordeaux of an unfamiliar vintage but, I thought, perhaps twenty-five years old. It was the classic unlabelled decanter trick, played on me by a friend whose father had been stationed in Chile. The bottle was the last of his hoard, so my estimate of its age may have been approximately right; the label was gone. The wine was a Cabernet Sauvignon, quite possibly from Cousiño Macul or Concha y Toro – the two most fashionable suppliers of the time (so I was told). It was very good indeed; warm and vigorous despite some fading with time, growing (as all very fine wines eventually do) gently sweet in its maturity.

I was very intrigued, and started investigating what Chilean wine could be bought in England. As far I could discover (this was in 1969) there was only one supplier. The now-defunct firm of Woolley, Duval and Beaufoys was shipping a Cabernet the old way – in oak hogsheads to bottle it in London. I tasted it and ordered a hogshead – to bottle myself. (I reckoned on a saving of a shilling or so a bottle.)

The arrival of that cask is a memory I shall always treasure. The lorry that brought it out to our house in the country was equipped with a driver and a porter who stood in relation to other men much as brewers' dray horses do to a regular saddle-horse.

With huge confidence they slung a noose of rope round the barrel, lowered it to the ground, then took a turn round the axle of the lorry and and started to lower the cask (it looked monstrous) in its sling down the external steps of my cellar, just as pubs take delivery of the necessary. One of the draymen paid out the rope above, the other stood arms akimbo in the cellar, standing guard over an old tyre at the foot of the steps designed to give the barrel a soft landing.

Something went wrong. The barrel slipped in its sling, turned on the steps and crashed down the last six. It bounced on the tyre and crashed again on the brick floor, smashing bricks with its iron-hooped end, and coming to rest like a great boar felled in the hunt, gently bleeding beautiful Cabernet from between its staves.

Luckily the lower drayman was a fast mover, or he too would have been bleeding, if not squashed flat. With admirable presence of mind he seized a mallet and chisel and set to work like a cooper, driving the loosened hoops back tight onto the belly of the barrel. 'Silly boogers,' he said, 'shouldn't never of sent out cask without soaking 'em. Where's water?'

By the time he had finished tightening the hoops, swaddled the barrel with wet sacking and poured buckets of water over it the bleeding had eased to a trickle here and there. We had only lost, I suppose, four to five gallons of wine; a delicious-smelling puddle on the cellar floor. 'Keep it wet,' the drayman said. 'Silly boogers.' It had never occurred to me that a barrel of wine could be dry enough on the outside for the hoops to become loose. But then I suppose not many barrels are launched through the air to land with such impact.

What followed was more peaceful. I gave the wine a week to settle, only removing the bung and stirring in an antiseptic solution of sulphur tablets in water. Then I set about the joyful task of bottling it, syphoning it through a rubber hose that always needed another little suck to keep it flowing. The party lasted four days, during which I kept running out of bottles and bothering my friends for any container they could spare. There was *far* more in a Chilean hogshead than my calculations allowed for. The price per bottle plummeted and my spirits soared. I had never tasted such a wonderfully luscious, prime, plump and promising wine. From that time on Chile became for me a Promised Land.

My first arrival in Chile was on foot, in the snow, as part of a detachment of dendrologists (the word describes those whose love of trees exceeds the normal, and perhaps even the rational). We were exploring the forests of Patagonia, and the pass seemed a good place to leave the bus and go for a walk – in this case from Argentina to Chile. We were not disappointed. This is not the volume in which to detail the giant Eucryphias and Weinmannias that greeted us as we entered the forest zone. But I thought the name of the latter species had distinctly encouraging overtones.

A week of winemanship followed this 1975 visit to southern beeches and monkey-puzzle forests. The week confirmed what I already knew: that Chile's Cabernet Sauvignon is one of the earth's great natural resources.

I learned that the Bordeaux cuttings originally brought to Chile in the 1840s had always grown on their natural roots; that phylloxera, that curse of almost all the world's vineyards, had never crossed the Andes to infect Chilean soil (and also that if it did the Chilean method of flood irrigation would probably be capable of drowning the louse.) Whether it is fanciful to attribute the distinctiveness of Chile's Cabernet to the plants being whole and ungrafted I cannot tell. Yet there is something wonderful in the fact that a new vineyard is made simply by burying long canes of vine-wood half their length deep in the ground.

On the negative side, I learned that years of political and economic difficulties had left the Chileans without the means to acquire new equipment, up-to-date presses or, above all, new barrel wood. The oak that is needed for first-class cooperage does not exist in Chile. Most bodegas have been forced to make do and mend, cleaning and patching their old barrels as best they can. There comes a time, though, with not-very-skilled labour using inadequate tools, and the barrel needing more and more sulphur each year to disinfect it, when it ceases to be an effective and hygienic container. The wine from it (though perfectly healthy to drink) picks up taints that its regular drinkers get used to, but strangers find off-putting.

This problem is more serious with white wines than red. Combined with a traditional Spanish-style taste for white wines stored a long time in wood, it makes clean and fresh white wine the exception – available only where a bodega has concrete vats, or has been able to afford the still-rare stainless steel.

In 1975 these problems were acute – and the best wine-producers were actually aware of them. But I have been to other wine countries with endemic difficulties and left depressed. Not so with Chile. I left glowing, inspired to tell the world what perfect grapes were growing, and how little apparently needed changing to turn them into perfect wine.

This book is the account of a second journey to the vineyards of Chile ten years later – this time in the company of Jan and Maite Read, with whom my wife and I have shared several memorable journeys in Spain.

There were many differences about this second visit – perhaps the greatest being that we had the help of the Chilean authorities. Yet it is sad to report that, in any comparison with any other wine country of comparable potential, Chile has not made anything like ten years-worth of progress.

While the leading Chilean wine-makers are now fully aware of international standards of wine-making, it is still, with rare exceptions, only in the making of their splendid Cabernet Sauvignon that they can match them. There is so much that adequate investment could achieve so quickly that it is impossible not to feel frustrated for knowledgeable and ambitious individuals and well-run companies baulked by forces beyond their control.

The evidence on which these conclusions are based is the subject-matter of this book. Each sample that has arrived from Chile since our visit has encouraged the feeling that problems are being overcome. About the potential of Chile to produce some of the world's most splendid wines nothing needs proving. We wait, and taste, in hope.

Hugh Johnson

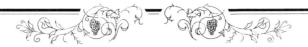

CHAPTER ONE

Surprises of a Long, Thin Country

Chile is a perpetual surprise, a country of contrasts, parts of which, at the same time, contrive to look very much like rural England or the Highlands of Scotland. To begin with, it is some 3,000 miles long, but only an average 100 miles wide, over which the land falls steeply from 20,000-ft peaks in the Andes to the cactus-ringed coast of the Pacific. The torrid deserts of the north give way, first to a smiling central valley, a Garden of Eden where almost anything – including, of course, the vine – grows and flourishes, then to a pine-covered region of lakes and mountains, and finally to the bleak wastes of Chilean Antarctica.

If it were less far – from Europe the flight takes some twenty-four hours, and from New York about twelve – it might well become a tourists' paradise. There are endless unspoiled beaches; splendid fishing in river, lake and sea; good riding and skiing; and, in the north and centre, more or less unbroken sunshine for most of the year. Yet, because of the nearness of the mountains and the cool Humboldt Current which washes its coast, the temperature falls rapidly at night, and it is rarely sticky or overpoweringly hot. Having travelled half way across the world, even the most single-minded wine enthusiast will want to see more than vineyards and wineries.

Apart from the perpetual vista of the Andes, snow-capped for most of the year – and rising sheer behind Santiago, the fifth largest city in South America with its population of some four million – the astonishing beauty of Chile lies in the luxuriance of its trees and flowers. Although the rose is not the national flower, it might well be so, for it runs riot in even the humblest peasant garden; and in the more temperate parts of the country, the dusty dirt tracks which

do service for roads are lined with wild dog roses (their hips are the basis of a thriving industry for making rose-hip syrup). The yellow broom flares far and wide like a torch, and such reminders of home are interspersed with more exotic blooms: the brilliant red trumpets of the copihue (which *is* the national flower), the sky blue of jacarandas, the pink oleander with its olive green foliage and the fiery red blossoms of the pepper trees, and cactus flowers in every hue and shape.

The surprising thing about the trees is that foreign varieties outnumber the native. The country is lined with tall ranks of poplars and aromatic groves of eucalyptus, while great weeping willows hang over every water-course (they are, for some reason, all male and do not propagate naturally, but are individually planted.) Among the more spectacular collections of trees are those in the parks of the Cousiño family, wealthy owners of mines and vineyards, near Santiago and at Lota in the south, both laid out by a nineteenth-century English landscape architect. The cedars of Lebanon in the park at Santiago are probably the tallest and finest in the world. Fruit is one of Chile's largest exports, and there are huge plantations of oranges, lemons, apples and avocado pears (or *paltas*, as they are known there) – and almost everything else, except for bananas, which are imported.

Considering the country's centuries'-long Spanish heritage, one thing that will strike a visitor from Europe is the almost entire absence of historic buildings. The central districts of the large Chilean towns and cities are entirely modern in character, with anonymous high-rise blocks – if you want to study old Spanish missions and churches, you must go to Peru or California. The most obvious reason for this is the occurrence of earthquakes. These are normally mild – it is not unusual to feel a gentle shock in one's hotel room at night – but against

the recent severe earthquake in Santiago and those of 1822, 1835, 1868 and 1875 in other parts of the country the buildings of the colonial period, often constructed of *adobe* (or dried clay) stood little chance. Such of the older churches as survive are stone-built with a wooden steeple, replacing one that was destroyed. This said, and despite the existence of numerous low-built *casas de campo* with tiled roofs, pilastered verandahs and flowering patios, the Chileans display little reverence for the legacy of their Spanish forbears and describe *any* building dating from forty years or more as 'very old'.

Chile is divided, not into provinces, but into large administrative districts numbered I to XII from north to south. The best of the wines are produced in the Metropolitan Region around Santiago and in the VI and VII regions to its south (*see fig. 1, p. 40*), within easy reach of the capital by road or rail. If you wish to venture further afield, northward to explore the deserts and beaches of Arica or to investigate the production of fiery pisco around La Serena, or again to visit the spectacular lake district in the south or to ski in Chilean Antarctica, the best way of travelling is by air. There are numerous internal flights: by the excellent LAN-Chile, the national airline; by the privately owned Ladeco, which for slightly higher fares offers really first-rate service and meals; or by one of the smaller airlines. An attraction of flying is that it is the best way to gain an impression of the Andes, as the planes follow the line of the mountains, only a few thousand feet above the snow-covered gullies and chasms, or the craters of far from extinct volcanoes.

For shorter journeys, Chile has an extensive railway system. Much of it was constructed by that nineteenth-century colossus of the railroads, the American William Wheelright — is this, perhaps, why the tracks are everywhere bordered by brilliant sheets of the orange Californian poppy? There are now no passenger services north of Santiago, but during the late nineteenth century Chile was often at loggerheads with its northern neighbours, Peru and Bolivia, and for this reason one is always encountering now-disused strategic lines, sited well away from the coast and snaking away at near-impossible gradients into the mountains. The main trunk line from Santiago to the south has been electrified. Despite the broad gauge, the antique but comfortable coaches bounce like boats at sea; but, as an alternative to flying, it is well worth taking the night train to Valdivia and places south, equipped with surprisingly comfortable sleepers of German vintage dating back to the early 1900s, with the berths arranged lengthwise for a smoother ride.

The main wine centres south of Santiago, Rancagua, San Fernando, Curicó, Talca and Chillán, are well served by train, but it is simpler to go by car down the Pan-American Highway, a wide and uncluttered

Opposite

Wooden church tower in a village above the Elqui valley

19

road with stretches of double carriageway, spanning Chile from north to south. Since the country is so narrow, it is never more than an hour's drive east or west of the Highway even to the furthest vineyards or wineries.

The wineries welcome visits; it is, for example, the policy of Viña Undurraga to open its *bodegas* and park to the public throughout working hours. At smaller concerns a knowledge of Spanish is more or less essential if one is to understand the guide, but a big firm like Viña Concha y Toro employs a uniformed English-speaking hostess (smartly turned out in a man's evening jacket and bow tie), who will smilingly escort you around the cellars and pour the wines in the elegant tasting room. Here they sometimes stage displays of traditional dancing for larger parties, the hostess, now in costume reminiscent of Andalucía, heading a team drawn entirely from the firm's employees. Not to be outdone, another of the big wineries, Viña Santa Carolina, has been known to engage a top-flight group of singers to regale its guests, not only with its wines, but with folk music and jazz.

Details as to the location of the leading wineries will be found in

Lombardy poplars in the vineyards near Cauquenes

Fisherman at Tongoy

The cactus-fringed coast
near Coquimbo

Opposite
Bavarian-style tower, wood
with painted brickwork, in
Vicuña

Top
Old Colonial-style house at
Totihue

Bottom
Colonial-style mansion of
the Undurraga family

The international observatory at Tololo, 7,000 ft up in the Andes and the most important in the Southern Hemisphere

Chapter 7. It is possible to visit many of them simply by making day or half-day excursions from Santiago. It is in itself a beautiful city, with the glittering and ever-present backdrop of the Andes. Particular attractions are its many wooded parks and open spaces, the residential quarters with their luxuriant gardens and the great fish and fruit markets. For wine-lovers, there is the Enoteca perched half way up the 1,000-ft hill of San Cristobál, rising dramatically from the centre of the city. This houses a permanent exhibition of Chilean wines, with free tastings of the 'wine of the day' and a restaurant with magnificent panoramic views of the city below.

There is a wide range of hotels and restaurants at all prices, of which particulars may be obtained from the Servicio Nacional de Turismo,

Catedral 1165 (Tel. 82151), opposite the Congreso Nacional. Visitors are strongly recommended, nevertheless, to obtain a copy of *The South American Handbook*, published annually by Trade and Travel Publications, Bath, England, which contains up-to-date information about hotels and restaurants, together with a great deal of detailed and practical advice about travel arrangements and what to see and do in Chile generally.

Hotels in the larger towns and in resorts and seaside places, of which the largest is Viña del Mar near Valparaiso, are clean and comfortable, and often modern. No special health precautions are necessary as in the countries in the tropics of South America, though it is sensible to have a typhoid injection; and to avoid tummy upsets visitors should be careful about salads and strawberries, or other fruit grown in contact with the ground, and drink bottled water.

Younger vintages of estate-bottled wines sell at £1 or less in shops and supermarkets, and the most expensive old *reserva* costs no more than £3.50, though you will pay considerably more in restaurants and hotels. Another attraction for visitors is the superb shellfish from the cold waters of the off-shore current. Details of the cuisine and of typical dishes will be found in Chapter 8. And a last word before embarking on an account of the wines: after a hot day in the vineyards or on the beach, try a glass of Pisco Sour as an apéritif. Pisco and its uses in making cocktails are also described later.

The observatory buildings at Tololo

25

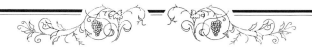

CHAPTER TWO

A Little History

The history of wine-making in Chile begins with the conquest and settlement of the country by the Spaniards. Until the first expedition in 1530 of Pizarro and his lieutenant, Almagro, the country was only sparsely inhabited by native Indians; and it took years of bitter fighting before the next of the Conquistadores, Pedro de Valdivia, occupied the north and centre, founding the city of Santiago in 1541. Even he was unable to subjugate the south and was captured and tortured to death by the fierce Araucanian Indians.

Viticulture was first introduced by the Catholic priests who accompanied the Conquistadores, so as to provide wine for the sacraments. An early chronicler, The Abbot of Molina, relates that he found the black Moscatel growing wild in the foothills of the Andes near Curicó, so that it is possible that the vine was native to Chile. However, the first vine to be cultivated and used for wine-making was the black País, known elsewhere on the continent as the Criolla and in California as the Mission. According to tradition it was first brought to Chile by the Jesuit, Father Francisco de Carabantes, in 1548, but accounts of its origin vary. Some say that it was brought directly from Spain or from the Canary Islands, and others that the first vines were grown from the pips of raisins, a staple food of the Spanish sailors. Certain it is that it flourished and spread, and it is still the predominant variety, especially in the south, though it is no longer used for making the more select wines.

The names of some of the earliest wine-makers have survived: it is on record that Don Francisco de Aguirre planted vineyards at Copiapó in the north, first harvesting them in 1551, and that by 1554 Don Juan Jufré possessed extensive vineyards near Nuñoa to the south-east of Santiago. All the early historians agree that the soils and climate were exceptionally favourable for growing vines and making wine.

In his *Vista general de las continuadas guerras y difícil conquista del Gran Reino y Provincia de Chile*, Tibaldo de Toledo wrote that 'Santiago is the most flourishing garden in the world, surrounded by olive groves and vineyards and making good and abundant wine'. Diego de Rosales, another great historian of the colonial period, described the region around Maipú as 'one vast garden producing wheat, barley, maize, beans, peas and lentils, together with a multitude of trees and an infinity of vines, producing excellent wines'. Again, the Jesuit Alonso Ovalle, writing in 1646, commented on 'the famous wines, of which the best and most reputed are the moscatels' and added a note of warning, still applicable in more recent times: 'They have killed many of the Indians, who drink without restraint, since they are so strong as to rot their entrails.'

A century later, Vice-Admiral John Byron, grandfather of the famous Lord Byron, or 'Foul-weather Jack' as he was nicknamed by his sailors, was wrecked off Cape Horn in 1740 and subsequently succeeded in making his way to Santiago with a handful of survivors. In his book, *The Narrative of the Honourable John Byron*, published in 1768, he wrote: 'The estancias, or country houses, are very pleasant, having generally a fine grove of olive trees, with large vineyards to them. The Chili wine, in my opinion, is full as good as Madeira.' He also notes what is still true today, that it was 'made in such quantities that it is sold extremely cheap. The soil of the country is so fertile, that the husbandmen have very little trouble; for they do but in a manner scratch up the ground, and without any kind of manure it yields an hundred fold'.

Another generation of British soldiers and sailors was soon to play a decisive role in events which were to change the whole course of the country's history and not least the fortunes of the wine industry. At the period of the Napoleonic Wars, Chile, like the rest of the Spanish colonies in South America, was still rigidly controlled from Madrid. Discontent was rife among the creoles, native-born Americans of Spanish descent, who bitterly resented the appointment of *peninsulares* from Europe to all the key administrative positions and, beyond this, the iron restrictions on agriculture and foreign commerce. So, a British naval commander, Captain Basil Hall, reports in his *Extracts from a Journal written on the Coasts of Chili, Peru and Mexico*, published in 1824, that:

Even so late as 1803 . . . orders were received from Spain to root up all the vines in the northern provinces, because the Cadiz merchants complained of a diminution in the consumption of Spanish wines. I was informed at Tepic of a measure precisely similar having a few years earlier been carried into effect in New Galicia, in the case of some extensive and flourishing tobacco plantations. The Americans were prevented, under severe penalties, from raising flax, hemp, or saffron. The culture of the grape and olive was forbidden, as Spain was understood to supply the colonies with wine and oil. . . .

No South American could own a ship, nor could a cargo be consigned to him; no foreigner was allowed to reside in the country, unless born in Spain; and no capital, not Spanish, was permitted in any shape to be employed in the colonies. Orders were given, that no foreign vessel, on any pretext whatever, should touch a South American port.

In Chile, events came to a head in 1810, when the Spanish Captain-General was deposed and a Junta of seven leading citizens assumed power in Santiago. It was hardly to be expected that the Spanish authorities would accept this *coup d'état*; civil war broke out and was fought with varying fortunes, the patriot forces being under the command of John MacKenna, an Irishman and professional soldier who had taken service with the Spanish, and Bernardo O'Higgins, also of Irish descent and the son of Ambrosio O'Higgins, another important officer of the Spanish Crown in Peru.

Britain took no official part in the hostilities, but, as the leading mercantile country of the day, it was clearly in her interest to see an end to restrictions on trade, and no serious attempt was made to stem the flood of British adventurers and mercenaries, many of them veterans of the Napoleonic Wars, who made their way to South America to fight on the side of the emergent republics.

O'Higgins was badly defeated at Rancagua in 1814, but took refuge with one hundred and twenty of his men in what are now the cellars of the well-known wine firm of Viña Santa Rita; he succeeded in escaping to Buenos Aires, where he joined forces with another patriot leader, José de San Martín, and made a triumphant comeback after the epic passage of the Andes by their army. One of his first acts after being named President of the new republic was to call on the services of Lord Thomas Cochrane.

A brilliant sailor, in disgrace with the Admiralty at the time for his unorthodox methods and opinions, Cochrane arrived in Chile in 1818 and straightway set about the creation of a navy. A motley fleet was assembled, made up of old men-of-war and armed merchantmen, which Cochrane manned with untried Chilean peasants and an extraordinary mixture of foreign mercenaries, many of them British.

With this unpromising material and in uneasy partnership with San Martín, he launched a series of daring amphibious expeditions, northwards to Peru, the seat of Spanish power in the west of the continent, and to the south of Chile. As a result, the last of the Spaniards were defeated in Chile in 1820, and Peru had largely been liberated by 1822.

Don Melchor de Concha y Toro, Marqués de Casa Concha, one of the founders of the Chilean wine industry

To this day, every town and city in Chile has its streets named after Bernardo O'Higgins, General MacKenna, Admiral Cochrane and his trusty English comrade in arms, General Miller, in recognition of their outstanding services. It is of interest that two of the country's leading wine familes, the Undurragas and the Eyzaguirres of Las Vascos, are direct descendants of General Mackenna.

The expulsion of the Spaniards led to much wider trade with the

Grape-gathering in the
Macul vineyard, near
Santiago. (Engraving from
the *Illustrated London News*,
5 Oct. 1889)

outside world of all the country's commodities – potash, copper, silver and gold, and agricultural produce, including of course, wine – and the settlement of foreign engineers and agriculturalists resulted in a stimulus to production. It was not, however, until the middle of the nineteenth century, with wealthy Chileans making the Grand Tour of Europe, that radical reorganization of the wine industry was begun.

In 1851, the visionary Don Silvestre Ochagavía engaged the first French oenologist to work in Chile, a M. Bertrand, and embarked on the replantation of his vineyards, replacing the traditional País with noble varieties brought from Europe, including Cabernet, Cot, Merlot, Pinot, Riesling, Sauvignon, Sémillon and the others from which fine wines are made in Chile today. He was joined in this by his father-in-law, José Tomas Urmeneta; Maximiano Errázuriz Valdivieso carried matters further by planting 300 hectares of foreign vines on his estate at Panquehue in the fertile Aconcagua Valley north of Santiago. When the vineyards were later extended to some 1,000 hectares by his son, they were the largest in the world belonging to a single proprietor.

Entrance to the Macul wine stores, Santiago. (Engraving from the *Illustrated London News*, 5 Oct. 1889)

Thanks to this suitability of the soil and climate, the foreign vines throve. It was also found that they were much less affected by diseases of the vine: for example, mildew and botrytis are virtually unknown in Chile.

It now became the fashion for the wealthy owners of coal and silver mines to vie with one another in bringing back noble vine stocks from their travels in Europe and in establishing vineyards and wineries.

In a book spanning the events of his long life, *Recuerdos de ochenta años*, Francisco Undurraga, painter, poet and politician, and great uncle of the present proprietor of the firm, Don Pedro Undurraga, describes the pains to which he went to bring back the precious Riesling stocks bought in Coblenz, Frankfurt and Cologne on a visit to Germany. Encased in metal tubes, they were kept under refrigeration so as to avoid budding during the long, hot voyage across the equator.

He was equally careful about the wood in which the wine was aged. On his appointment as overseer of the State Railways, he set about the purchase of much-needed equipment, ordering fifty locomotives from Germany and two thousand flat cars from Bosnia and Herzegovina. There was, perhaps, more than meets the eye in his choice of this seemingly unlikely source of supply, for, as he relates in his book:

> The wood from these parts is first class and very aromatic, and the Bosnian oak gives the wine a special fragrance, resulting, as the years go by, in a magnificent bouquet unobtainable with any other type of wood. For this reason it is used for sherry and port casks, which fetch enormous prices after long use in the large *bodegas*.

Wine-pressing at the Macul stores, Santiago. (Engraving from the *Illustrated London News*, 5 Oct. 1889)

Don Francisco was aware that the packing cases in which the railway equipment was shipped were broken up and sold for firewoood, and continues:

> I offered to buy the staves from the captain of the ship, but he was selling them very expensively. I then offered what I thought reasonable, but he rejoined that for that price he would rather use them for firewood on board. I then said: 'Let us ask for a couple of staves from Larios Hnos', and when these were to hand, I demonstrated that each of them was four times the size of his. 'You are right,' he said. 'I will give them to you at the price you have offered for firewood' – and he sold me the lot for ten thousand pesos. The barrels were subsequently made for me by the famous cooper L'erromau.

Most of the wineries founded at this period survive and are the famous names of today; their history is told in more detail in Chapter 7. They included: Viña Conchalí (José Joaquín Aguirre); Viña San Pedro (Bonifacio Correa Albano); Viña Cousiño Macul (Luis Cousiño); Viña Concha y Toro (Melchor Concha y Toro); Viña Lontué (J. Correa Errázuriz); Viña Santa Rita (Domingo Fernández Concha); Viña Carmen (Cristián Lanz); Viña Santa Teresa (Macario Ossa); Viña Santa Carolina (Luis Pereira) and Viña Linderos (Alejandro Reyes).

Not surprisingly, as the vineyards and wineries were founded by the Chilean élite, mostly of Basque descent, many of the wine familes are interrelated. It was the great grandfather of Don Pedro Undurraga, Domingo Fernández Concha, who founded Viña Santa Rita, building the house and laying out the gardens. On his death, the family sold the firm to cousins from whom it passed to the present proprietors. Again, Domingo Fernández Concha's mother was a daughter of Melchor Concha y Toro, founder of the famous firm of that name. Some of the firms are still linked by family ties: for example, the managing directors of Concha y Toro and Cousiño Macul are cousins.

One of the factors contributing to the growing prestige of the wines was that Chile escaped that most terrible scourge of the vine, phylloxera, which from 1863 onwards devastated the vineyards of Europe. This was probably because Chile is isolated by natural barriers: the vast deserts to the north, the snows of Antarctica to the south, the Andes to the east and the Pacific to the west. Whatever the reason, the insatiable phylloxera louse never penetrated the country, and to this day the vines are planted ungrafted without recourse to North American stocks. When the European vineyards were replanted it was, in fact, often with grafted *Vitis vinifera* from Chile. The outcome is that the flow of sap in the ungrafted Chilean vines is more fluid and their useful life runs to a hundred years, rather than the thirty or so in Europe and California. Again, the vines introduced into the country from France are pure-bred and the only examples in the world directly descended from the European vines of the pre-phylloxera period.

The period of the late 1880s was perhaps the most prosperous in the history of the Chilean wine industry, with production growing from 51,400,000 litres in 1875 to 110,300,000 litres in 1883. Their quality was reflected in exports and in the medals won in the international exhibitions of the time. They were first shipped to Europe by Don Macario Ossa of Viña Santa Teresa in 1877 and soon won recognition in France.

In his *Recuerdos*, Don Francisco Undurraga tells an amusing story about the first sale to the United States of his celebrated 'Rhin Undurraga' made from the thousand vines earlier brought from Germany. The Managing Director of the American Grace Lines, a Mr Ear, was staying with him at the time in 1903, and Don Francisco expressed a wish that he should buy sufficient cases to sell at least one in every State of the Union. Ear then wagered him a pound sterling that he

Opposite top
In the Cousiño park at Lota, near Concepción

Opposite bottom
In the Andes above the Elqui Valley

could not name half of them. Don Francisco, who had majored in geography, at once rattled off the entire list and the impressed and astonished Ear not only undertook to sell at least a case of wine in each of the States, but also put in a personal order for one thousand cases.

Foreign producers began to take stock of Chile as a serious competitor when the wines swept the board at the Buffalo exhibition of 1910, and one of the firms which capitalized on this and earlier successes was Undurraga, which still exports a larger proportion of its production than any other.

The subsequent story has not been so happy. Although production increased by leaps and bounds, the producers were unable to find a sizeable foreign outlet for their wines – other than in Latin America, where Chile has always been the major exporter.

A tax on wines and spirits, first levied in 1902, had a depressing effect on the industry. Known as the Impuesto de la Ley de Alcoholes (ILA), this currently runs at 15 per cent, and an added value tax or Impuesto de Valor Agradado (IVA) of 20 per cent is also levied. It is a common complaint of the larger firms that they face unfair competition from a host of moonlighters, who sell direct to the consumer, evading both taxes – and one has only to drive along the Pan American Highway to see a succession of billboards warning agriculturalists about such tax evasion. Wines for export are, however, free of tax.

Between 1938 and 1974, the plantation of new vineyards was virtually prohibited by law in an effort to stem the rampant alcoholism among the Chilean population; and the final blow was the attempt by the Allende regime to introduce agrarian reform at breakneck speed, so splitting up the larger properties among smallholders without the capital or the expertise to exploit them.

Perhaps the most pressing problem today is a lack of capital to modernize the wineries, many of which, especially the cooperatives, are thoroughly old-fashioned in their equipment. To a foreign observer, the most urgent need would seem to be the replacement of innumerable picturesque, but insanitary wooden vats and barrels, long past their useful life and actually detrimental to the wine which is aged in them.

A few facts and figures will illustrate the present scope of the Chilean wine industry. With a total annual production of $5\frac{1}{2}$–6 million hectolitres, it ranks twelfth in the world league, making about the same amount as Hungary or Bordeaux. The typical Chilean drinks almost 55 litres of wine per annum, putting the country sixth in terms of world consumption.

There are 5,864,100 hectares of land under cultivation, 2 per cent of it under vines. Of the 1,356,000 hectares of arable land which are

Opposite top
The Cordillera de la Costa near Cauquenes

Opposite bottom
Santiago, capital of Chile, founded by the Spaniards in 1541, but now a large and spacious modern city

irrigated, 4 per cent is given over to vineyards. Vineyard area has not varied a great deal over the last fifty years: in 1930 it amounted to 81,700 hectares, in 1938 to 104,000 hectares, and in 1958 to the present figure of 110,000 hectares.

There are some 33,000 growers, though most of them are small-holders, since only 3,000 own more than 4 hectares. Taking into account their families, it has been estimated that some 140,000 people depend directly for their livelihood on viticulture. The industrial and distributive sides of the industry employ another 15,000 workers, so that, all in all, families included, some 200,000 people or 2 per cent of the population are involved. Wine is therefore a most important part of the economy.

As a footnote to this short survey of the origins and development of the Chilean wine industry, it should be explained that there has never been any comprehensive legislation regulating the production of wine. In Europe and elsewhere, increasingly strict rules have been enforced as to the planting of vineyards, the composition of wines and the demarcation of wine-growing areas. Indeed, in some cases, this appears to have gone too far, as in Italy, where the creation of innumerable *Denominaziones di Origine Controllata* (DOC) for regions producing wines of indifferent quality has debased the currency. Chile stands at the opposite extreme; apart from certain regulations covering the manufacture of pisco (*see p.76*) and the export of table wines, wine-makers have been free to do exactly as they wished.

Matters are, however, on the move, and a new wine law has recently been enacted. Among other things, this requires the growers to notify the Ministry of Agriculture as to proposed new plantings, specifying the vine varieties; it forbids alcoholic beverages made from hybrid grapes to be labelled as 'wine', and calls for the establishment of *Denominaciones de Origen (Appellations d'Origine)*. At the moment, these are limited to pisco and to *pajarete* and *vino asoleado* (varieties of forti-fied wine). The demarcation of table wines presents difficulties, since the large wineries draw their fruit from widely different regions of the country. Nevertheless, the proposals of the new law are clearly a step in the right direction and are summarized in detail in Appendix 1.

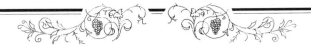

CHAPTER THREE

Soils, Vines and Vineyards

The regions

Vines are cultivated in Chile over a distance of some 600 miles, from Copiapó in the north to the River Cautín in the south. Not surprisingly, there are great variations of soil and climate.

There is no official classification of the different wine-growing regions, but the scheme put forwards by Don Rodrigo Alvarado Moore in his excellent book, *Chile Tierra del Vino*, has been generally adopted. In this, he distinguishes between irrigated zones, amounting to 65,000 hectares, and unirrigated (*Zonas de Secano*) amounting to 45,000 hectares. The irrigated zones, lying in the central valley and watered by the rivers flowing down from the Andes, produce the choicest wines. Alongside them, but further to the west in the more barren land of the Cordillera de la Costa, a mountain range running parallel to the coast, are the corresponding unirrigated zones, particularly suited to the País vine.

1. *Zona Centro Norte* (Central Northern Zone)

This region lies on the southern fringe of the arid deserts of the north in the large provinces of Atacama and Coquimbo. The vines are grown only in the valleys of the principal rivers, running laterally from the Andes towards the sea, and on the slopes of the smaller valleys of their tributaries. The most important is the Elqui Valley, debouching on to the coast at La Serena. Because of the almost entire absence of rain, especially in the north of the area, the vines must be irrigated. The brilliance of the light and the heat of the sun results in wines of high alcoholic degree and low fixed acidity. The area is planted almost exclusively with varieties of Moscatel, and the fruit from the

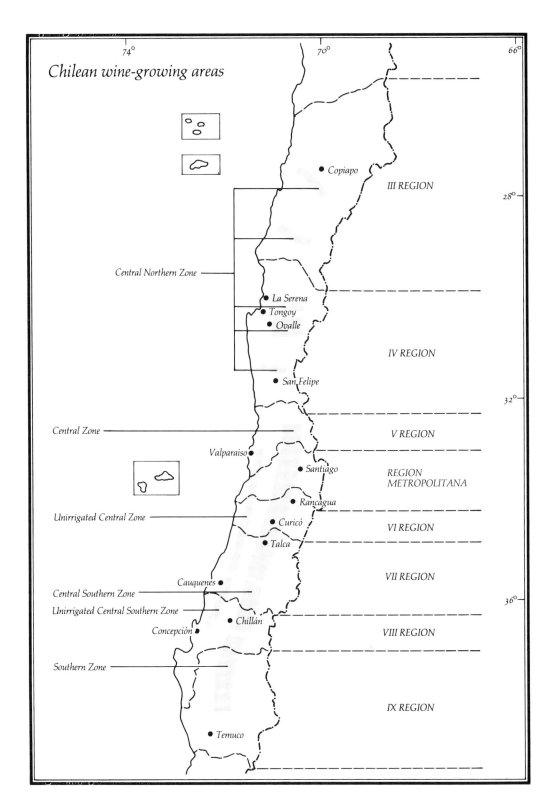

Chilean wine-growing areas

74° 70° 66°

Copiapo

III REGION

28°

Central Northern Zone

La Serena
Tongoy
Ovalle

IV REGION

San Felipe

32°

Central Zone

V REGION

Valparaiso

Santiago

REGION
METROPOLITANA

Rancagua

Unirrigated Central Zone

Curicó

VI REGION

Talca

VII REGION

Cauquenes

36°

Central Southern Zone
Unirrigated Central Southern Zone

Chillán

VIII REGION

Concepción

Southern Zone

IX REGION

Temuco

larger part (7,300 hectares) produces wine which is distilled as an aromatic native brandy, pisco (*see Chapter 6*). A further 3,100 hectares of more fertile land produces excellent dessert grapes.

2. *Zona del Valle Central* (Central Zone)

This is the heartland of Chilean wine production, lying in the broad central depression between the Andes and the Cordillera de la Costa and comprising all the irrigated areas of the V, VI and VII Regions (*see fig.1*) and the Metropolitan Region (the former provinces of Aconcagua, Valparaiso, Santiago, O'Higgins, Colchagua, Curicó and Talca). Although the Aconcagua Valley lies a little to the north, it is convenient to include it.

Average annual rainfall increases from 300 mm in the north of the zone to 730 mm in the south, and irrigation is usually necessary from November to May (the summer months in Chile correspond, of course, to winter in Europe and North America).

Of the 43,810 hectares or irrigated vineyards in Chile, 37,161 are located in this zone; with an average yield of 6,000 litres per hectare, they produce 50 per cent of the country's wine.

The best of all the vineyards are in the Maipo Valley, just south of Santiago, which produce the most famous of the red wines. Other areas growing black grapes of particularly good quality are Peumo, west of Rancagua; Nancagua, near San Fernando; Lontué and Molina, just south of Curicó; and Talca, further south. The Aconcagua Valley, descending from the highest peak in the Andes, is a region apart from others in the zone, lying north of Santiago beyond a range of arid hills – the road passes the battlefield of Chacabuco, where O'Higgins and San Martín defeated the royalists in 1817, and plunges through a long tunnel before reaching the fertile valley, open to cooling winds from the Pacific. The vineyards at Panquehue were once the largest in Chile, but 80 per cent of production from the valley is now of dessert grapes for export.

The zone as a whole is planted with the black Cabernet Sauvignon, Cabernet Franc, Cot, Merlot and Verdot, but smaller amounts of the white Sémillon, Sauvignon Blanc, Pinot and Riesling are also grown.

3. *Zona Central de Secano* (Unirrigated Central Zone)

This runs parallel and to the west of the Central Zone along the line of the Cordillera de la Costa and lies within the same administrative regions. It is bounded by the city of Viña del Mar to the north and by the line of the River Maule, flowing just south of Talca, to the south. There is sufficient rainfall in this hilly area to dispense with irrigation; it is mainly planted with the native black País and farmed by smallholders. The vineyards, amounting to 9,052 hectares and

Opposite
Fig. 1
Map of Chilean wine-growing areas

yielding an average 4,000 litres per hectare, produce 8 per cent of the national total.

4. *Zona de Valle Central-Sur* (Central Southern Zone)

Lying within the VII and VIII Regions and bounded by the River Maule to the north and the limits of the old Province of Nuble to the south, this irrigated zone, especially the northern part, is very similar in characteristic to the Central Zone. The rainfall is significantly higher and, oddly enough, the mean average temperature is also rather higher, though the extremes are much greater.

The same noble black grapes are grown, but the area is best known for its excellent white Sauvignon and Sémillon wines. With 6,649 hectares under vines and an average yield of 6,400 litres per hectare, it makes somewhat less than 10 per cent of the country's wine.

5. *Zona Centro-Sur de Secano* (Unirrigated Central Southern Zone)

The zone embraces the remaining vineywards in the VII and VIII Regions as far south as Concepción, planted on the slopes of the Cordillera de la Costa. Owing to an average annual rainfall of more than 1,000 mm, they are not irrigated and are planted almost entirely with the black País. In irrigated regions the País produces large yields of coarse wine, but in this zone, with yields often less than 3,000 litres per hectare, the quality is much better and the wine is pleasant enough for everyday drinking. Because temperatures are lower, the region also produces small quantities of good Riesling and Sauvignon Blanc wines, and a fragrant Moscatel.

The region is more densely planted with vines than any other in Chile. The vineyards extend to 45,000 hectares, and viticulture is the predominant agricultural activity. It is farmed by a host of smallholders, and there are large cooperatives at Cauquenes and Quillón to which they may take their fruit for vinification.

A recent study undertaken by the Experimental Station of the Instituto de Investigaciones Agropecuaries at Cauquenes has shown that with supplementary irrigation of some 200 mm per annum and modern methods of vineyard management and vinification, the Cauquenes area has the potential to produce both red and white wines from the classical grapes as abundantly as the Central Zone. That it cannot do so at the moment is because of lack of investment and the need to educate the smallholders in modern techniques.

6. *Zona Sur* (Southern Zone)

Opposite
Fig. 2.
Map of Natural Divisions

This embraces all the vineyards in the VIII Region south of Concepción and in the IX Region as far as the River Cautín. Further south, the climate is not mild enough to grow vines, and the Southern Zone

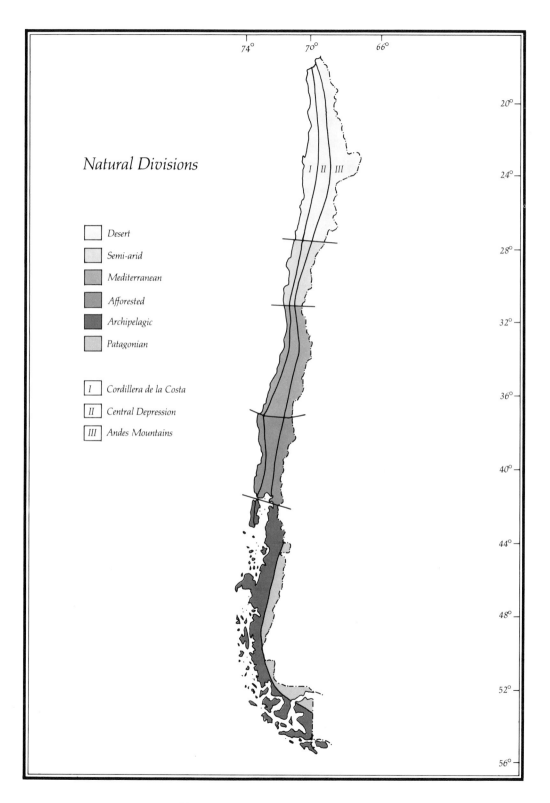

Natural Divisions

Desert
Semi-arid
Mediterranean
Afforested
Archipelagic
Patagonian

I   Cordillera de la Costa
II Central Depression
III Andes Mountains

itself is only marginally viable. Although it still possesses 8,282 hectares of vineyards, viticulture is on the decline, since wine of better quality is produced so abundantly in the more northerly zones.

Soils and climate

The schematic cross section of Chile in the region between Santiago and Talca (*Fig. 4*) shows that the central valley forms a great basin, into which, over the ages, a mass of debris, in places more than 300 ft deep, has been carried down from the mountain chains that flank it. The soils are therefore young in geological terms, not older than the period of the last glaciers and sedimentary in character, with inclusions which account for specific and localized variations.

Studying the fertility of a range of soils between Coquimbo and Curicó, Rodriguez and others (1977) found low levels of inorganic nitrogen, corresponding to a paucity of organic material. On the basis of nitrogen, phosphorus and potassium content, Rodriguez and his collaborators established a sequence of fertility levels for the different types of soil, listing them in descending order of fertility as follows:

Opposite

Fig. 3

Maps showing average annual rainfall and temperature

Dam near Ovalle

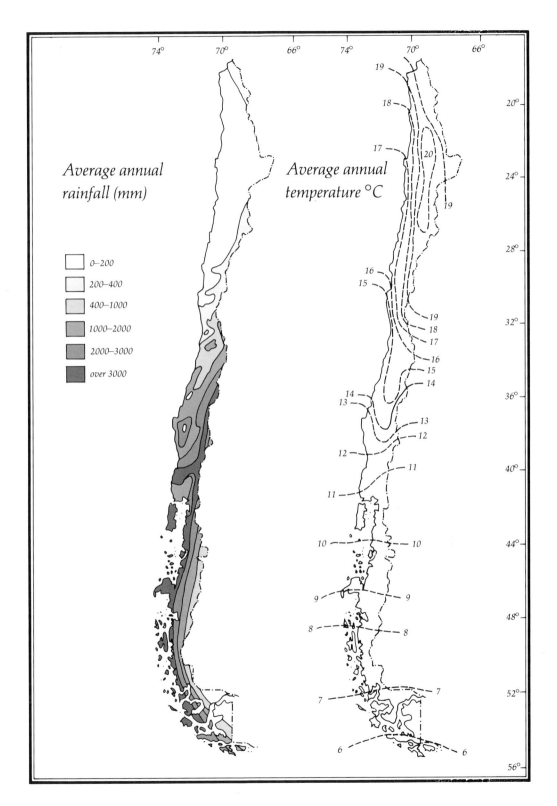

Average annual
rainfall (mm)

0–200
200–400
400–1000
1000–2000
2000–3000
over 3000

Average annual
temperature °C

lacustrine (lakeside) clays; fine-textured alluvia; granitic deposits; medium and coarse-textured alluvia; marine clays, marine sands; and hillside granitic.

In practical terms, the best wines are made from grapes grown in widely occurring soil made up of limestone, clay and small stones, allowing for good drainage, and in the alluvial silt and sands of the river margins. In parts of the Cordillera de la Costa, as around Cauquenes, the soils are predominantly granitic.

Figure 3 illustrates the wide variations of temperature and rainfall over the country as a whole; the wine-growing areas lie between latitudes 30° and 37° south, where differences are much smaller. In broad terms, the climate of the Central Valley may be described as Mediterranean; there are, however, important differences.

Because of the proximity of the Andes, with peaks rising as high as 23,000 ft and snow-covered even in summer, masses of cold air flow down into the Central Valley during the night, so that even in high summer, though temperatures rise to 30–35°c during the day, they fall to 10–15°c at night.

Another factor is the influence of the cold Humboldt current, which flows off-shore in the Pacific. Cool air from the ocean sweeps inland, tempering the summer heat. The flow is most pronounced in the Central Southern and Southern Zones, where the mountains of the Cordillera de la Costa are lower than in the Central Zone, and also in wide valleys running down to the sea, like that of Aconcagua. Around Cauquenes, temperatures, in fact, approximate to those of the Napa Valley and Sonoma County in California and are more or less ideal for viticulture.

The virtual absence of cloud or rain during the growing season and at harvest time results in a brilliance of light which profoundly affects the life cycle of the plants. Don Miguel Torres, who owns vineyards both in the Spanish Penedès and in Chile, has, for example, noted that in the Penedès Central the vines bud at the end of March and are ready for harvesting at the end of September, a span of six months. In the Central Valley of Chile, on the other hand, budding

Fig. 4
Schematic cross-section of
the Central Valley

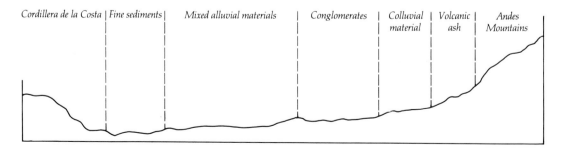

begins in mid-September and harvesting takes place in late February or early March, covering a period of five-and-a-half months. The combined effect of steep diurnal temperature gradients and high luminosity is both to shorten the growing period and to promote the formation of polyphenols – tannins and colouring matter – and also the elements responsible for the aromas of the fruit. It is for these reasons that grapes such as the Riesling and Gewürztraminer, best grown in the colder regions of Europe, yield splendidly aromatic wine when grown in the warmer climate of Chile.

Rainfall, varying from 300 mm in the north of the Central Valley to 730 mm in the south, is insufficient for viticulture, and the vines are therefore irrigated. This presents no problems in the Central Valley, since a series of rivers fed by the snows of the Andes – the Mápocho, Maipo, Rapel, Tinguiricia, Teno, Lontué, Mataquito, Maule and Nuble, to name only the larger – flows across the Valley on the way to the Pacific. Their waters are diverted into an extensive network of irrigation channels, so that the vineyards can be watered as required. Naturally, this is done only during the earlier part of the growing season, and not later, when it would result in dilution of the musts.

Irrigation is not carried out in the Zona Centra-Sur de Secano (*see*

Espalderas in the Peumo vineyards of Concha y Toro

p.42) because of the absence of suitable rivers in the Cordillera de la Costa. However, the Experimental Station at Cauquenes has carried out trials with drip irrigation, watering the vines individually from perforated rubber tubes. The results have been highly successful; after a period of four years, yields increased from 5,220 kg/ha to 21,550 kg/ha. Since there are reservoirs in the area and electrical power for pumping is available, it would seem that great advances in viticulture are possible, given imaginative planning and adequate investment.

Vine varieties

With the exception of the País, all of the vines cultivated in Chile are varieties of *Vitis vinifera* introduced from Europe from 1851 onwards. They are grown ungrafted, since Chile never suffered from the phylloxera epidemic of the late nineteenth century.

1. Black grapes

País

The origins and history of the País have already been described (*p.26*). It is a grape which does well in the unirrigated zones of the Cordillera de la Costa; when irrigated, it fruits more prolifically, but the quality of the musts is much poorer. Resistant to diseases, it yields wines which mature rapidly without much colour or body. About 35 per cent of all Chilean wine is made from the País. Of this, the larger proportion is the rough *vino 'pipeño'* (*see p.56*) or the popular *'chicha'* – a partially fermented must tasting much like raspberry vinegar (*see p.55*). Better table wines made with the País account for some 15 per cent of consumption.

Cabernet Sauvignon

This aristocrat from Bordeaux has adapted extremely well to the soils and climate of the Central Valley, where it is always irrigated. It is the basic grape for all fine red Chilean wines and is planted to the extent of some 12 per cent. The quality of the musts is quite exceptional, and when a party of foreign oenologists visited Chile some years ago, one of them went on record as saying that if ever a 'Cabernet Producers Association' was formed, Chile deserved the presidency.

Cabernet Franc

Closely related to the Cabernet Sauvignon, the Cabernet Franc is employed in conjunction with it, usually in the proportion of 1:9.

Cabernet Sauvignon vineyard at Peumo, showing the careful specification of the vines

Cot, Merlot and Verdot

Used together, these three grapes give rise to what are known commercially in Chile as *vinos 'Burdeos'* ('Bordeaux'). As in Bordeaux, the Merlot ripens more quickly than the Cabernet and is sometimes blended with it to give a softer, fleshier wine. The three varieties (the Cot is a synonym of Malbec) account for 7.5 per cent of production.

Carignan

This native of the French Midi has been grown in the unirrigated zones as an alternative to the País. Its wines are somewhat superior and deeper in colour. However, it is more prone to disease, and when irrigated it makes a dull wine.

Pinot Noir

The famous Burgundian grape is not widely grown in Chile because of the low yield, though one or two of the wineries, notably Undurraga, make a good Pinot. When fermented *en blanc* (without the skins or pips), it makes the best of the Chilean sparkling wines.

2. White grapes

Moscatel

The sweet Moscatel exists in Chile in various varieties. Apart from red Moscatels, the principal white varieties are known locally as the Moscatel de Alejandría, Moscatel de Austria, Moscatel itálica, Moscatel blanca, Moscatel amarilla, Moscatel de Canelli, etc.

It was cultivated even in colonial times, when it was the main source of white wines and is now much grown in the Zona Centro Norte (*see p.39*) for making pisco and also as a dessert grape. In the Zona Centro-Sur de Secano (*see p.42*), it produces fragrant white table wines.

At present it accounts for not more than 1 per cent of all white wines.

Sémillon

In admixture with the Sauvignon Blanc – and the two are often grown mixed in the vineyards – the Sémillon produces 87 per cent of Chilean white wine and is used both for everyday wine and fine whites. The vines are irrigated, and yields are higher than for any other variety.

Sauvignon Blanc

Vinified on its own, the white Sauvignon produces some of the most fragrant and delicate of Chilean white wines. The best of both these varieties are grown in the Zona del Valle Central-Sur.

Chardonnay

Outside its native Burgundy, the Chardonnay crops sparsely in Chile, and there are barely 100 hectares in cultivation. The wines are of excellent quality, lighter than most, with an intensely fruity and perfumed nose.

Riesling

The Riesling is also somewhat rare in Chile, though the Rhin Undurraga, made from vines brought to the country from Germany by the founder of the firm and aged in oak, was the first Chilean white wine to achieve a reputation outside the country. As vinified in stainless steel by a firm such as Torres (sometimes in combination with Gewürztraminer), it is a light and fruity wine of great delicacy. Although most of the vines are from the Rhine (Riesling Rhenano), one also encounters less delicate wines made from the Italian Riesling.

Cultivation

In the rural and unirrigated districts of the Cordillera de la Costa, planted mainly with the País, the vineyards are typically small and farmed by a host of independent farmers. The vines are grown low and unsupported, and pruned *en cabeza*, a method leaving three main branches each bearing two shoots, which produce twelve bunches of grapes in all. It resembles the *poda en vaso* of Spain, from which it was no doubt derived.

In the Central Valley, viticulture still reflects the methods employed in Bordeaux in the mid-nineteenth century and introduced by the oenologists who were brought from France at the time to supervise the planting of European vines and the making of the wines. It is, for example, common practice to effect *coupage* by planting different varieties of vine in the same plot in the proportions of the blend used in the wine. So, one finds vineyards in which two Sémillon plants alternate with one Sauvignon Blanc, or, in the case of red wines, Cabernet Sauvignon interspersed with Cot or Merlot.

The holdings of this area are much larger. The biggest of the Chilean wine firms, Viña Concha y Toro, owns an estate of 3,000 hectares at Cachapoal near Peumo, of which 2,000 are planted with vines. Here, as in other modern vineyards, the different varieties are grown separately, and a plantation of, say, Cabernet Sauvignon may extend to 40 hectares or more. It is not usual, however, as in the case of Cousiño Macul, for the big wine concerns to grow all their own fruit, and much is bought from independent farmers.

The traditional method of growing the vines, borrowed from Bordeaux, is in *espalderas*. In this method, two, four or more shoots are trained on wires supported by posts. These may be some 80 cm high, as in Bordeaux, or as much as 2 m, with yields, depending on the height of the *espaldera*, varying between 10,000 and 20,000 kg/ha. The traditional density of plantation was between 6,000 and 10,000

Examples of different vine varieties at the Pirque bodegas of Concha y Toro

vines per hectare, but the Chileans have been much influenced by Californian practice, and the tendency is now to plant the rows some two to three metres apart with one metre between the vines, so facilitating the use of tractors, but reducing the density of plantation to between 3,000 and 5,000 vines per hectare.

In recent years the *espaldera* has often been replaced by another system of training, the *parronal* (also known as the *parral* or *parrón*), introduced from Argentina and making possible huge yields of 400 or 500 hls/ha. The stakes and wires are higher, and the vines form a dense canopy of leaves on top, with the bare stems below. When the system was first introduced, it was claimed that it would much increase yields without affecting the quality of the wine. This has not proved to be the case. The dense layer of vegetation on top results in different temperatures and degrees of humidity, and especially in the case of noble varieties such as the Sauvignon Blanc and Cabernet Sauvignon, disagreeable herbal aromas may be produced in the grapes.

During 1978 to 1979 grapes grown by the *espaldera* and *parronal* systems fetched the same prices and were indiscriminately mixed, but now that the difference in quality has become clear, they are being vinified separately and producers are paid more for grapes from the *espaldera*.

As has already been noted (*p.34*), Chile was never affected by that most disastrous infirmity of the vine, phylloxera, a disease caused by a minute aphid, which feeds on the roots, producing incurable lesions. Except in a few other regions, such as Colares in Portugal and the French Carmargue, also unaffected by the epidemic, vines all over the world are now grafted on to American stocks resistant to the attacks of the insect. One of the benefits of Chile's freedom from the disease is that vineyards may be planted simply by taking shoots from existing vines and inserting them into the soil. Since the new plant is all of a piece, the flow of sap is freer; the plants are entirely *sui generis* and both healthier and longer-lived.

Plant diseases in general are less of a threat in Chile than elsewhere in the world. Mildew (*Phlasmopara vinicola*) and botrytis are virtually unknown. There is some incidence of oidium (*Uncinula necator*), a fungal disease affecting the leaves and buds, and this is combated by dusting with sulphur from the time of budding until late spring. The most common insect pests are the *arañita roja* (*Brevipalnus chilensis*), a tiny spider, and the *burrito* (*Panthomorus*), which, like oidium, attacks the leaves. Both are fairly easily controlled with suitable insecticides. More damaging is another insect, *Margarodes vitis*, which attacks the roots, causing lack of vitality and sometimes destroying the plant. It is especially prevalent in the Maipo Valley, and an effective means of combating it has yet to be discovered.

Opposite
Parronales at Viña San Pedro

52

The tending of the vineyards throughout the year parallels that in other countries; in the vineyards of the smallholders it is still carried out by hand, while the large concerns make increasing use of tractors and mechanized aids. As elsewhere, it includes ploughing around the roots so as to aerate the soil and collect the winter rains; application of fertilizer or manure during the winter; pruning in the early spring; light tillage to remove weeds during the late spring, and the control of diseases or insect pests during the growing season by dusting or spraying with suitable preparations.

Harvesting

Harvesting begins in late February or early March (the Chilean autumn) according to the situation of the vineyard, the vine variety and the ripeness of the fruit. Mechanical harvesters have not yet been introduced. The traditional method, still used by the smallholders, is to pick the grapes into wicker baskets and to empty the contents into large wooden tubs for transport to the bodega or, as is often the case nowadays, to the local cooperative.

A refinement of this method at Cousiño Macul employing all the resources of Victorian technology, is charmingly portrayed in the *Illustrated London News* of 5 October 1889. The pickers in the vineyards at Macul are shown loading the grapes into the tubs, which were then placed on a trolley and delivered straight to the heart of the bodega by a narrow-gauge track running from the vineyard. The track, alas, no longer exists and the fruit is now taken to the vinification plant in plastic-draped trailers hauled by a tractor.

Whether delivered to a cooperative or to a private bodega, the subsequent procedure is the same. On arrival, the fruit is checked, weighed and sampled for sugar content, and then tipped into a hopper and conveyed by a *tolvo* (or Archimedean screw) to the crusher.

There are two potions drunk far and wide in Chile at harvest time by the grape-pickers and the public in general: *chicha* and *vino pipeño*.

The word '*chicha*' is probably Quechuan, originating with the Incas, and the *chicha* drunk by the Indians was made by chewing maize and spitting it into a receptacle with water, when the mixture began to ferment. What is known as *chicha* today is a good deal more attractive and hygienic and is simply partially fermented grape juice, or must. It therefore varies in strength according to the degree of fermentation. If it has only begun, the *chicha* is very sweet and is known as *chicha crudo*. It is a fruity enough drink – reminding one of raspberry vinegar – but should not be drunk to excess, because as Rodrigo Alvarado Moore has amusingly remarked in a collection of essays, *Los Motivos del Vino*, 'fermentation may well continue in the stomach of the con-

Opposite top
Irrigation canal on the estate of Viña Canepa

Opposite bottom
Espalderas in the Central Valley

55

sumer, and it is hardly necessary to describe the consequences'.

In an attempt to stabilize the fresh *chicha*, it is sometimes heated so as to concentrate the must and increase the proportion of alcohol. In this case, it is known as *chicha cocida*; unfortunately, heating alone rarely achieves the desired effect, and the itinerant *chicheros*, or *chicha*-sellers resort to antiseptics of secret and highly dubious nature. Whether you are offered 'genuine' *chicha* of Curacaví, Lampa, Quilicura, Aconcagua or Villa Alegre, you have been warned!

Viño pipeño is simply new wine, which has not undergone filtration or clarification in any form. It therefore contains all the dead yeasts, together with solid residues from the grapes. As Rodrigo Alvarado Moore wrily observes, if fermentation has not been strictly hygienic, it will also contain other impurities 'beginning with soil and ending with other unsuspected ingredients better left undescribed'. Unless you know your wine-maker, it should again be approached with caution.

The river Cachapoal near Peumo

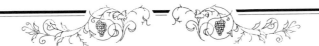

CHAPTER FOUR

Making and Maturing the Wines

Chile is best known abroad for its red wines, made principally by the methods introduced by the French oenologists who settled in the country during the mid-nineteenth century and set up the bodegas. There have, of course, been developments, and a major influence has been the training of a new generation of young Chilean oenologists in California.

Until the last few years, the white wines were fermented in wooden vats or in cement *depósitos* and then aged in oak. The turning point here was the arrival in Chile in 1978 of the skilled Spanish wine-maker, Miguel Torres, who subsequently set up a bodega equipped with temperature-controlled stainless steel fermentation tanks, so making possible the production of light and fruity white wines in the modern style. His example was followed by other large and enlightened firms, and the whole style of the white wines is currently changing in favour of the new-style whites, so much more saleable in foreign markets than the traditional and often maderized wines.

Vinification of red wines

With few exceptions, most of the large wineries were constructed in the late nineteenth century and their layout resembles that of the châteaux of Bordeaux at the time or, perhaps more closely, that of the large bodegas in the Rioja, also French-inspired, but with a continuing emphasis on the long-term ageing of the wines in oak vats and casks. Many, like those of Concha y Toro, Cousiño Macul and Undurraga, with their endless cellars and rows of wooden containers of all shapes and sizes, are buildings of great beauty and character. The

Stainless steel tanks at the Maipo winery of Concha y Toro

vaulted underground cellars of Viña Santa Carolina have, in fact, been declared a National Monument.

On arrival at the bodega, the grapes are fed into a hopper and conveyed by means of an Archimedean screw to a crusher, which at the same time removes and rejects the stalks. A little sulphur, usually in the form of potassium metabisulphite, is added to inactivate undesirable yeasts, and the must, containing the skins and pips, but not the stalks, is pumped into the fermentation vats, leaving space at the top to allow for frothing. In some of the older bodegas, fermentation is still carried out in *cubas* ((large receptacles made of oak or raulí, a species of South American beech), but standard practice, both in the private wineries and in the cooperatives, is to use concrete vats (or *depósitos*) coated with vitrified epoxy resin. Tumultuous fermentation, during which the grape sugar is broken down into alcohol and carbon dioxide gas, normally takes place at 28–30°c and lasts for about three days, during which the cap or *sombrero*, formed of skins and solid matter carried to the top by the vigorous evolution of gas, is at intervals broken up and redistributed.

The aroma and fruity flavour of a red wine are improved by vinifying it at temperatures nearer 25°c, and at its impressive new winery on the outskirts of Santiago, Viña Canepa achieves this by vinifying the must in large stainless steel tanks fitted with an internal coil, through which refrigerant is pumped to obtain any desired temperature. Made in California, the tanks are reinforced with stout ribs to safeguard them against earthquakes.

Once vigorous fermentation is complete, the new wine is left for another week or so, then pumped off into large wooden or concrete vats to complete more gradual malolactic fermentation and to settle for some months before being transferred to smaller receptacles to begin the process of maturation. The wine at the bottom of the fermentation vat is mixed with skins and pips, from which it is freed by pressing, either in the traditional upright basket press with slatted wooden sides or in the newer types of horizontal press used for white wines. The *vino de prensa* or press wine is darker and much richer in tannins than the wine first drawn off the fermentation vat, and at the discretion of the oenologist a proportion is blended with it to achieve better balance and longer life.

The lighter *claretes* are vinified in the same fashion as the fuller-bodied *tintos*, except that the skins and pips are left in contact with the fermenting must for a shorter period, so that less of the tannins and colouring matter pass into the wine.

Stainless steel tanks at the bodegas of Viña Canepa, ribbed to withstand earthquakes

Vinification of white wines

Chilean white wines were traditionally vinified in the same fashion as the red, except that the must was first freed from the skins and pips. In most cases this was done in old-fashioned 'continuous' presses, which, by bruising the stalks, skins and pips, left bitter and tannic elements in the wine. A refinement was to employ a horizontal press, which with an arrangement of plates and chains squeezes out the must more gently through the slatted sides.

Whatever the method of pressing, fermentation in wood or cement vats at temperatures approaching 30°c resulted in the loss of aromatic and flavouring elements – hence the advantage of temperature-controlled stainless steel tanks. Apart from being easily cleaned and more hygienic, they make possible much slower fermentation at temperatures around 15°c, so conserving the volatile substances in the wine.

Since Miguel Torres first introduced such stainless steel vats at his winery near Curicó in 1979, the large concerns of Concha y Toro, Santa Carolina and Canepa have all invested heavily in similar equipment, and Viña Santa Rita is following suit. Cooling may be affected either by running cold water over the outside of the tank or by an internal coil, and in the most modern installations it is possible simply to set the required temperature on the dial of a console. Whatever the method of cooling, the use of such equipment makes possible the retention of all the most delicate aromas and flavours of the grape

Below left

Pressurized tanks for making sparkling wine by the *cuve close* method at Champagne Subercaseaux

Below right

Cooling element inside a modern fermentation tank at Viña Canepa

– hence the emergence of 'generic' wines made from a particular grape variety, such as Sémillon, Sauvignon Blanc, Chardonnay or Riesling.

The stumbling block is the heavy capital investment. Although Chile is a large producer of iron and steel, there has been no concern capable of making the tanks, which have been imported from Catalonia or the United States.

Vinification of rosé wines

Rosé or *rosado* wines are made from the must of red grapes, usually the Merlot or Cabernet Sauvignon. According to the degree of colour and body, the must is left in contact with the skins for periods ranging from minutes to a day or two and is then fermented *en blanc* (without the skins and pips), like white wines.

Vinification of sparkling wines

Chile does not make much sparkling wine. The largest producer, Valdivieso, makes a certain amount by the original Champagne method, and some of the other firms, such as Santa Carolina Undurraga and Concha y Toro, produce limited quantities by the Charmat or *cuves closes* process. In this, a suitable white wine (usually a Chardonnay or Pinot Noir, vinified *en blanc*) is dosed with sugar and cultivated yeasts and undergoes a second fermentation, not like Champagne in individual bottles, but in pressurized stainless steel tanks. As in the

Bottles awaiting filling at Viña Santa Rita

case of Champagne, the bubble is produced by the breakdown of the added sugar into carbon dioxide and alcohol.

At Santa Carolina there are eight of these tanks of 20,000 litres capacity, used at harvest time for making still white wine. At other times of year, they are pressurized to five atmospheres, and the wine, white or rosé, with its quota of sugar and Épernay yeasts, undergoes a second fermentation for some twenty-two to twenty-six days at 15°c and is then bottled under pressure.

For making its good 'Subercaseaux' sparkling wines, Concha y Toro has installed a battery of refrigerated tanks, specially designed for the purpose and thickly lagged to maintain low temperatures.

Another and inexpensive type of sparkling wine is made as at Viña Manquehue, simply by cooling white wine and passing into it carbon dioxide from a cylinder.

Unlike the producers of *cava* in the Spanish Penedès – which *is* made by the Champagne method – the Chilean producers are not trammelled by any agreement with the producers in Rheims, and both the *méthode champenoise* and *cuves closes* wines are uninhibitedly labelled as 'Champagne'.

Don Pedro Undurraga amid his casks

Ageing

Both the red and the traditional white wines are aged in wood. After a period of months, the new wine is racked (or decanted off the lees) and transferred to a fresh receptacle, the importance for the red wines of the period in wood being that they undergo slow and controlled oxidation from air entering through the pores and also pick up tannin and flavouring elements, notably vanillin. The net result of a complex series of chemical reactions is that the wine gains both in complexity of bouquet and flavour. The older red *reservas* are aged for three to four years in wood, first in large barrels or *fudres* and then in smaller casks – though few are as small as the 225-litre cask used in Bordeaux or the Rioja.

The best wines are matured in oak; some of the original casks, made from wood imported from Bosnia, have survived, but the newer oak is mainly from the United States. However, the great bulk of the recipients, especially the larger, are made from a native hardwood, raulí (*Northofagus procera*), a species of beech growing in southern Chile.

The problem arises that many of these containers have remained *in situ* since the bodegas were first constructed. They are, of course, washed out and disinfected either by burning a sulphur candle or with sulphur dioxide gas, before receiving a fresh batch of wine. Over the years, the older have nevertheless accumulated a layer of tartrate, blocking the pores and thus negating the purpose of ageing in wood. Further than this, it is extremely difficult to wash away traces of sulphur dioxide absorbed by the wood of the larger fixed *cubas* and *fudres*. Investigations carried out by the Wine Department of the Universidad Católica in Santiago have shown that the residual sulphur dioxide (SO_2) combines first with water to form sulphurous acid (H_2SO_3), which may then be oxidized to sulphuric acid (H_2SO_4). The net result is to render the wine which is stored in them unacceptably sharp and acid.

Red wines can only benefit from a period in healthy wood, but if the wood is too old and insanitary, the best young wine will suffer. Too often one has tasted a well-made and splendidly fruity young wine, which has subsequently gone downhill in a sixty year-old raulí vat. The long-term solution is to replace the older wooden receptacles; short of this, it would seem preferable to dispense with wood in the case of wines made for early consumption and to rest them in stainless steel tanks or epoxy-coated cement vats prior to bottling.

It is no longer the fashion to age white wines for extended periods in wood, though there is still a following in Chile for such wines, which to foreign tastes seem excessively oaky and, in some cases, maderized (i.e. oxidized and sherry-like). Some white wines benefit

Old Casks in the cellars of Concha y Toro at Pirque – note the distinctive oval shape

from a short period in clean oak, and these, too, are to be found – a good example is the nicely balanced 'Bellaterra' from Torres. Fortunately, in the case of the increasingly popular new-type white wines, no problem arises with the wood, since they are not aged in oak, but simply refrigerated and then centrifuged or filtered to remove sediment before bottling.

Given the magnificent quality of the *materia prima* and the skill of Chilean oenologists, the main problem facing the wine industry is the capitalization of a programme for modernizing the older wineries and, in particular, renewing the wood, installing stainless steel and coating existing cement vats with resistant epoxy resin. This was something which the authors preached during their visit to Chile, and since then the leading concerns have spent some US $2,000,000 on just such improvements.

Bottling

The maturation of a red wine does not end with its time in wood; wine is a living material and gains in flavour and intensity from a period in bottle, although more slowly, as a result of a complicated series of chemical processes, both of oxidation and reduction. For fine wines, the modern tendency is, in fact, to cut down the period in wood to a year or two and to extend the time in bottle. All of the

major wineries have underground storage space running to millions of bottles for this purpose.

For some reason, bottles are always in short supply in Chile and are commonly returned, as were the old lemonade bottles nearer home. In fact, the first thing to meet the eye outside many of the Chilean wineries is the huge pile of bottles and carafes of every shape and size, which are duly sorted, washed, sterilized and re-used.

Everyday wines are sold in 1-litre bottles or 5-litre carafes. Those used for the fine wines are of four types: the round-shouldered Bordeaux bottle; the Burgundy bottle with sloping shoulders; the tapering 'flute' bottle of the Rhine; and the *caramayola*, a flagon similar in shape to the German *bocksbeutel*. This last type has always been used by Undurraga for exporting its wines – though not for those sold domestically – and some other firms have followed its example. In almost all cases, the bottles hold 700 ml and not 750 ml.

Despite the extensive flora, the cork oak is not grown in Chile, and corks are imported from Spain or Portugal. They range in length from 30 mm to 40 mm for the less expensive wines to 45 mm for the better.

As elsewhere, bottling and labelling are carried out on a mechanized line or *tren*, the most deafening part of any winery, but because it is often the most modern, the one where visitors are encouraged to linger!

Casks in the cellars of Santa Carolina

65

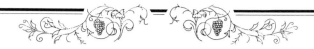

CHAPTER FIVE

Into the Glass

Classification of Chilean wines

At this point it is usual to print a list of vintage years, but it should be explained that the climate in Chile is so benign, and one summer is so like another, that there *are* no vintage charts – and consequently none of those handy plastic cards to help one choose the best wine at a moment's notice.

The problem of choosing a wine is compounded by the absence of any system for demarcating the table wines (*see p.38*). At basic level, everyday drinking wine, corresponding to *vin ordinaire* or *vino corriente*, is sold in 5-litre carafes or litre bottles, but beyond this it is a question of trusting to the label and the reputation of the maker – hence the witty remark of that doyen of Chilean wine writers, Don Rodrigo Alvarado Moore, that the Chileans drink labels, not wine. He comments further that the information on the label is usually cryptic enough, being confined to the name of the producer, his address, the volume of contents, the percentage of alcohol, the term '*producto chileno*' and 'a fanciful name or possibly a reference to a grape variety or region which does not always correspond to the truth'.

To help in the understanding of the labels, I follow his guidelines:

1st Category
These wines are usually named after a member of the aristocracy or carry a name preceded by 'Don' or 'Doña'. They may also carry the names of precious metals or be described in terms of superlatives, e.g. 'Marqués de Casa Concha', 'Don Maximiano', 'Finisimo'.

They are carefully selected, vinified at the winery and matured for three or more years in American oak and at least one in bottle. The reds are made with 100 per cent Cabernet Sauvignon from the Central Valley, and the whites with a blend of Sémillon and Sauvignon Blanc from the same zone.

2nd Category
Also carrying aristocratic names, but generally of lesser nobility, these wines are similar to those above, but younger, e.g. 'Don Luis'.

3rd Category
This group comprises the bulk of the wines of good middle-of-the-road quality – and some have been judged better than the wines of the first two categories in international exhibitions. The reds are made with Cabernet Sauvignon, blended with a proportion of the 'Bordeaux' varieties (Merlot, Cot and Verdot), and the whites with a blend of Sémillon and Sauvignon Blanc. The Rieslings are not usually 100 per cent varietal.

4th Category
Confusingly enough, the wines of this group are labelled '*Gran Vino*'. This is a legacy of the days when the producers were compelled to sell certain wines at official prices, pegged at artificially low levels. To avoid this, they evolved the description '*Gran Vino*' to describe young wines of good quality. The reds are usually of the 'Bordeaux' type made from a blend of Merlot, Cot and Verdot, e.g. 'Panquehue Gran Vino Tinto Cosecha 1981', and the whites young Sémillon-Sauvignon wines.

   All of the above types are sold in 700-ml bottles, while those of the 5th Category are marketed in litre bottles or 5-litre carafes.

5th Category
These comprise wines, often cooperative-made, of average or below-average quality, made from the País grape and blended with press wine from the noble varieties. The whites are made from lower-quality Sémillon and other grapes, or from País musts vinified *en blanco* (i.e. without the skins and pips).

Characteristics

The above classification is clearly of limited use and reflects traditional Chilean taste – namely that the oldest wines are necessarily the best. Wine waiters almost always recommend the oldest (and most expensive) wines on the list and are surprised if, in the light of personal preference, one opts for something younger. In the case of the white wines it is nevertheless true that, with the emergence of fresh young varietal wines, opinions are changing.

Tasting at Concha y Toro

It has long been recognized that the best of the Chilean Cabernet Sauvignons, intense and fruity, with very marked varietal nose and long finish, can hold their own with most. It should, however, be stressed that the wines mature more rapidly than their European or North American counterparts. There are wines like the glorious 1972 'Antiguas Reservas' from Cousiño Macul which are still at their peak; but without special knowledge it is, as a general rule, better to choose a younger wine rather than a ten year-old. The reasons for this quicker development are probably because the hot summer sun produces less acid in the grapes and because the yield per hectare is higher than in Europe.

Another factor has been touched upon already (*p.63*): if a fruity young wine is aged in old and imperfectly clean raulí containers, it will worsen rather than improve and become prematurely acid. For these reasons, the red wines of intermediate age (corresponding to Categories 2, 3 and 4) are often more to the foreign taste than the old *reservas*. Naturally, this is very much a question of how a particular wine has been aged, and the reader should consult the tasting notes of Chapter 7.

As regards the white wines, the position is very much as it was in the Rioja some years ago, when the Spanish taste was for oaky and somewhat maderized wines and the bodegas began making cold-fermented wines in the light and fruity modern style. There will always, one hopes, be a following for the well-made traditional whites,

like the Undurraga 'Viejo Roble' or 'Reserva de Familia' from Viña Santa Carolina, with their nice balance of oak and fruit. However, it has become clear that the future lies with the new-style wines, so that, as far as the whites are concerned, the five categories are now largely irrelevant. A wine like the cold-fermented Torres 'Bellaterra' gains spice and flavour from a few months in oak, but in general the new varietal whites do not see oak and depend upon their youthful freshness and the quality of the fruit for their appeal. The best of them are light and crisp, with fragrant nose and good fruit, and excellent of their kind.

Maite Manjón tasting at Concha y Toro

Keeping, decanting and serving

Chilean wines – even the old *reservas* – are so modestly priced that it is well worthwhile laying down a selection if you have cellarage. Before buying one of the older red wines for this purpose, it is advisable to taste it to ensure that it is not past its peak and, of course, to open a bottle at intervals to check its development. The wines with the most potential for improvement are the rather younger reds; and one should look for those with sufficent tannin rather than a softer and more immediately drinkable wine – the fruity 1981 'Don Matias' from Cousiño Macul, though somewhat harsh when tasted in November 1984, is a good example.

Red wines should be served at room temperature and, as a general rule, be opened about an hour before serving so as to air them. They do not normally need decanting, as the older wines have already thrown their deposit in cask, and the younger do not call for it.

The traditional oaky whites are best when slightly below room temperature, and the new-style wines should be drunk young and chilled. Some of them smell a little of sulphur when first opened, so draw the cork ten minutes beforehand to get rid of any bottle stink.

Labelling

The words and phrases most commonly found on labels are as follows:

Antigua reserva	Mature wine of good quality, aged in oak for three or four years and further in bottle.
Brut	Dry, used only of sparkling wines.
Cepaje, Cepaje noble	Vine variety, noble vine variety.
Champaña	Sparkling wine, made by the *cuves closes* process or *méthode champenoise*.
Cosecha	Vintage, e.g. Cosecha 1977 or Año de Cosecha 1977.
Elaborado por	Produced by.
Embotellado en origen	Bottled at the winery.
Embotellado por	Bottled by.
Envasado por	Bottled by.
Fundada en	Founded in.
Grado alcohólico	Alcohol content. Grado alcohólico 11.5 GL means that the wine contains 11.5 per cent by volume of alcohol.
Gran Vino	A young wine of good quality, probably three to four years old.
Reserva	Mature wine of good quality, aged for some years in oak and also in bottle.
Sirvase frío	Serve cold.
Viña	A wine firm, e.g. Viña Undurraga.
Viñedo, Viñedos propios	Vineyard, grown in the company's vineyards (estate-grown).
Vino	Wine.
blanco	white.
clarete	light red.
dulce	sweet.
rosado	rosé
seco	dry.
tinto	full-bodied red.

Opposite
Pisco vineyards in a valley
high above the Elqui

70

Exports

From colonial times onwards, Chile has always exported its wines to the other countries of Latin America. Shipments in more limited amount to the USA and Europe date from the last decades of the nineteenth century (*see p.34*). Its best customers have traditionally been Brazil, Argentina, Colombia, Venezuela and Costa Rica.

Patterns are, however, changing. Wine production has been increasing by leaps and bounds in Argentina, where the main centre of production is in the Province of Mendoza in the shadow of the Andes, only 150 miles west of Santiago. This area alone possesses two and a half times as many vines as Chile and half of all those in South America. Although in the past the emphasis has been on quantity rather than quality, there has been heavy investment in modernizing the wineries and in planting better vine varieties. One of two of the wineries are now producing very nice Cabernet Sauvignon, and the Chilean producers will have to look to their laurels.

Brazil, again, traditionally a large importer of Chilean wines, is making efforts to establish a wine industry.

Chile currently exports only 5 per cent of its production, and in view of the high quality and modest price of the wines, there is clearly great scope for expanding exports outside Latin America – with the added advantage that they will earn sorely needed hard currency, both to pay for imports and improve living standards. The main thrust is in the direction of the United States and, to a lesser extent, Europe. Figures for the production and shipments of the leading exporters follow, and a breakdown of exports to foreign countries will be found in Appendix 2.

EXPORTS FROM LEADING PRODUCERS – 1986

Winery	Vineyard area (ha)	Capacity in wood	Capacity in cement vats (hl)	Capacity in stainless steel (hl)	Exports (cases)
Coop. Agr. de Curicó Ltda	1,414	7,183	202,850	—	6,397
Coop. Agr. de Talca Ltda	1,160	60,000	140,000	—	5,000
Miguel Torres (Chile)	150	945 barricas	1,500	7,500	22,629
Viña Canepa	493	61,500	51,000	62,000	18,862
Viña Concha y Toro	1,391	229,620	282,680	11,000	416,147
Viña Cousiño Macul	264	54,300	26,200	—	50,105
Viña Errasuriz-Panquehue	140	28,000	37,000	1,500	16,583
Viña Los Vascos	185	13,322	8,270	265	26,585
Viña San Pedro SA	330	78,000	220,000	—	148,875
Viña Santa Carolina SA	—	173,000	86,000	2,500	71,560
Viña Santa Rita	145	43,000	245,000	1,100	69,523
Viña Taracapá	70	30,000	—	—	3,789
Viña Undurraga	195	21,500	68,900	—	75,412

Opposite top
Alfresco lunch at Pisco Control, Ovalle

Opposite bottom
Copper stills for distilling pisco

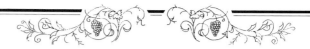

CHAPTER SIX

Spirits and Fortified Wines

PISCO

On the commercial scale, Chile produces no brandy in the French style, though there seems no reason why it should not; we have drunk a 'Quinta Normal', made experimentally by the Facultad de Agrónomia of the Universidad de Chile in Santiago, which was light, dry and fragrant in the manner of a good Armagnac.

The spirit universally drunk, especially at Christmas, is pisco. Like brandy, it is distilled from wine, and annual production runs to some four million cases. It takes its name from 'Pisku', which in Quechua, the language of the Incas, means 'flying bird' – a good description of this volatile liquor, light, dry, aromatic and water-white. It is usually drunk chilled with mixers – especially with fresh lemon juice as 'Pisco Sour' or with the local papaya juice – and given adequate promotion, there seems no reason why it should not compete with spirits such as vodka, gin or tequila.

The Pisco Region

Pisco is produced in the Andean valleys of the III and IV Regions, lying between Santiago and the deserts of the north. These (from north to south) are the valleys of the Copiapó, Huasco, Elqui, Limarí and Choapa, of which the most important are those of the Elqui and Limarí.

Shut in by the arid ochre heights of mountains devoid of all vegetation, roofed by an arching blue sky as intensely blue as the lapis lazuli from their mines and bathed in a brilliance of light which hurts the eyes, the valleys have an unearthly aspect. The people, too, seem a race apart. The Diaguitas, farmers and potters of renown, were overrun by the Incas in 1430, and they in their turn fell to the Spaniards; and negro slaves and Mapuche Indians from the south have contributed to this melting pot of cultures.

Nobody better than a Nobel Laureate, the poetess Gabriela Mistral, has captured the quality of the Elqui Valley, where she was born:

> . . . an heroic cleft in a mass of mountains, so short as to be no more than a torrent with green banks; yet small as it is, one comes to love it as perfect.
>
> It contains in perfection all that man could ask of a land in which to live: light, water, vines and fruit. And what fruit! The tongue which has tasted the juice of its peaches and the mouth which has eaten of its purple figs will never seek sweetness elsewhere.
>
> Wherever there is a hump, a ridge or bare patch without greenery, it is because it is naked rock. Where the *Elquino* has a little water and three inches of soil, however poor, he will cultivate something: peaches, vines or figs. That the leafy, polished vines climb only half way up the mountainsides is because, if they were planted higher, they would wither in the pitiless February sun. . . .

As a literary footnote to this sketch of a fascinating area, it is interesting to speculate whether La Serena at the mouth of the Elqui Valley on the Pacific, an elegant town built in neo-Colonial style, or the adjacent port of Coquimbo, with its deep anchorage and jetties for loading mineral ore, may not have been the setting for Joseph Conrad's novel, *Nostromo*. It is sometimes stated that he had in mind Guayaquil in Ecuador, but this stretch of the Chilean coast would seem to correspond exactly. The Gulf of La Serena (his Sulaco) is always shrouded by clouds in the morning, as in the book; there is a (now-disused) railway to the silver mines at the top of the valley – one still encounters trucks laden with gold ore rumbling down the narrow road; and finally, Nostromo, that redoutable *capataz de cargadores* in charge of the dockers, was Italian. It so happens that there is a strong Italian element in La Serena.

Viticulture

The soil is light, stony and alkaline, and temperatures are very high, though falling steeply at night. With over 300 cloudless days in the year, the luminosity is so high and the atmosphere so clear that the largest astronomical observatory in the southern hemisphere has been constructed at Tololo ('the cliff of the condors') on a 7,000-ft peak overlooking the Elqui Valley.

The vineyards, extending to 7,200 hectares, are planted in the valley bottoms, and since the average annual rainfall is only 120 mm, falling in the winter months of June, July and August, they must be irrigated. Conditions such as these result in high concentrations of sugar in the grapes, and the musts are more suitable for distillation than for making table wines. The vines were traditionally planted Bordeaux-fashion in *espalderas* (*see p.51*) with yields of between 10,000 and 15,000 kg/ha, but between 1975 and 1981 all the new plantations, amounting to 2,500 hectares, were of the Argentinian *parronal* type (*see p.52*), giving very high yields of between 25,000 and 40,000 kg/ha.

The Pisco Region was for long the only one in Chile to possess an official *denominación de origen* (*appellation d'origine*), and the authorized grape varieties are:

Moscatel Rosada or Rosada Pastilla
Moscatel de Alejandría or Blanca Italia
Moscatel de Austria
Torontel
Pedro Jiménez

The most aromatic pisco is made from Moscatel de Alejandría or Moscatel Rosada, for which the distilleries pay a 15 per cent premium. A further 3,100 hectares of Thompson Seedless are also grown, but only as a dessert grape.

Elaboration

The grapes are first destalked and crushed, but are fermented in contact with the skins and pips, so as to preserve as much as possible of the

Stills for making pisco at
Pisco Capel in Vicuña

aroma and flavour of the Moscatel grapes. Fermentation takes place in large concrete vats and normally lasts for some five days at 28–30°c. There are Chilean oenologists who maintain that a more fragrant product would be obtained by fermenting at lower temperatures, and experiments are being undertaken in this direction. The must, containing some 12–14° of alcohol, is next transferred to large tanks of between 1,000 and 2,000 hl, to undergo secondary fermentation and for suspended matter to settle out, before passing to the distillery.

Distillation is carried out discontinuously in copper stills of the Charentais type at 90°c, only the middle fraction or 'heart', consisting of some 70 per cent of the distillate, passing forward for elaboration as pisco. The first and last fractions, the 'heads' and 'tails', are blended with fresh wine and redistilled.

At this stage, the middle fraction contains some 55–60 per cent of alcohol by volume and is diluted with water to between 30 and 43 per cent of alcohol, depending upon the grade of pisco for which it is destined. The spirit is then matured in vats or casks of oak or raulí of various sizes and for periods of between two and twelve months, according to the quality and type of the final product.

The different grades of pisco are:

Gran Pisco	43°
Reservado	40°
Especial	35°
Selección	30°

The stronger the spirit, the more time it spends in oak; and a propor-

Distillery of Pisco Control at Ovalle

tion of the pisco aged in smaller oak casks is blended with the less alcoholic varieties. The 'Selección' is fruity with an aromatic nose reminiscent of bitter almonds or plums; the stronger varieties are oakier, drier and more elegant. All are water-white and transparent.

Pisco may alternatively be bottled with lemon juice as a ready-to-drink Pisco Sour, or by steeping in it fruit such as plums or apricots, used for making attractively dry liqueurs.

The Pisco industry

Pisco has been made in the region since the early days of the Spanish conquest, but until the 1930s it was produced in a host of small private distilleries, to which the smallholders sold their wine, and the quality was very variable.

The law establishing a *denominación de origen* for pisco was enacted at the beginning of 1931 and was followed later that year by the foundation of the Cooperative Agrícola Control Pisquera de Elqui Ltda, an organization with the resources to employ modern technology and to produce a consistent product of high quality. With 444 members, who supply the grapes from their vineyards, and the capacity to distil 3,154,300 litres of wine monthly, it is the largest of the pisco concerns, and 'Control', as it is popularly known, is the biggest selling brand. Apart from a central plant and offices in La Serena, it operates two distilleries in the Elqui Valley, one of them in the historic old town of Vicuña. This centres on a square shaded by centuries'-old pepper trees, of which the main feature is a wooden tower painted with imitation bricks, erected in Bavarian style by one, Braun, a bird of passage who arrived from his native Germany to install electric power in the region and remained to become mayor. It is now a National Monument.

The firm's other four distilleries are in the Limarí Valley, in Huamalata, Sotaquí, Rapel and Tulahuén. Its labels comprise 'Pisco Control' (in the four different qualities of Selección, Especial, Reservado and Gran Pisco); 'Pisco Sotaquí'; 'Liquores Campanario', liqueurs made by macerating apricots (*damascos*), cherries (*cerezas*) or loquats (*nisperos*) in pisco; and 'Control Sour', one of the freshest-tasting of the bottled Pisco Sours, containing three parts of pisco to one of lemon juice, prepared from a concentrate of the natural juice.

Next in size to Pisco Control is the Cooperativa Agrícola Pisquera de Elqui Ltda, abbreviated to Pisco Capel. Its history parallels that of Pisco Control and began in 1942 with the formation of an Association of Small Producers of Elqui by some thirty smallholders, dissatisfied with the private distilleries. As one of its founders, the 83 year-old Don Ernesto Peralta of Paihuano, has remarked: 'The distilleries were trading on us. They paid what they liked, and we wended our way from one to another like drones with our baskets of fruit. It was a regular fandango! Things went well from the beginning, when we bought a house here in Paihuano for the headquarters of the Association and a distillery in the village of Diaguitas'.

In 1964 the Association converted itself into a cooperative and now numbers 425 members with a large plant on the outskirts of Vicuña distilling a hefty 1,500,000 litres of wine monthly. Its brands include 'Pisco Capel' in the usual four grades; 'Capel Sour', a bottled Pisco Sour; and also 'Pajarete de Elqui Huancara', a fortified white wine.

Between them, Pisco Control and Pisco Capel are responsible for some 70 per cent of the total production of pisco, and in 1983 they banded together with the two largest concerns further north, the Sociedad Agroindustrias del Huasco and the Cooperativa Agrícola y Pisquera del Valle de Copiapó Ltda, to form the Compañía Pisquera de Exportación Ltda. The purpose of this company, which operates from Santiago, is to promote the sales of pisco abroad. For this there is a clear need, since, with domestic sales currently running at 1,920,00 cases per year, excess production amounts to 913,333 cases.

There seems no reason why its efforts should not eventually suc-

The Elqui river

ceed, though a market survey in the USA has shown that American consumers, used to blander spirits such as gin and vodka for use with mixers, were somewhat disconcerted by its more aromatic character. The question much debated by the large producers is whether to continue along present lines or to modify their processes so as to make more neutral spirit for export markets – which, on the face of it, would seem a pity.

The complete list of pisco producers and their brands is:

Cooperativa Agrícola Control Pisquera de Elqui Ltda
'Pisco Control'
'Pisco Sotaquí'
'Liquores Campanario'
'Control Sour'

Cooperativa Agrícola Pisquera de Elqui Ltda
'Pisco Capel'
'Capel Sour'
'Pajarete de Elqui Huancara'

Agroindustrias del Huasco Ltda
'Pisco Río Huasco'
'Pisco Tongoy'

Cooperativa Agrícola y Pisquera del Valle de Copiapó Ltda
'Pisco Inca de Oro'
'Vino generoso Inca de Oro'

Cooperativa Agrícola Frutícola y Pisquera Monte Patria Ltda
'Pisco Río Limarí'

Agroproductos Bauzá y Cía Ltda
'Pisco Bauzá'
'Pisco Río Grande'

Agrícola Casaux Ltda
'Pisco Pablo Rodríguez'
'Pisco Cascaux'

Sociedad Agrícola Pisquera de Elqui Ltda
'Pisco Tres Cruces'

Cooperativa Vitivinícola del Norte Ltda
'Pisco John Barnes'

Opposite
Wooden church near Ovalle

Sociedad Agroindustrial San Ramón Ltda
'Pisco San Ramón'

Pisco Tacam Ltda
'Pisco Tacam'

Pisco Tres R Ltda
'Pisco RRR'

Sociedad Productora Pisco Diaguitas
'Pisco Diaguitas'

Sociedad Agrícola Peralta
'Pisco Peralta'

Sociedad Pisquera del Huasco
'Pisco Carmen del Huasco'

Mixed drinks with pisco

The most popular way of drinking pisco is chilled with fresh lemon juice, as Pisco Sour, and it is the most refreshing of apéritifs on a hot day. The lazy man's way is to resort to the bottled variety, but although this is made with lemon juice concentrate – and not with citric acid, as in the case of some bottled *sangrías* – it never has the verve of a Pisco Sour made with freshly squeezed lemons. A sweeter version popular in Chile is made by shaking the pisco with bottled papaya juice.

Here are some recipes from Pisco Control:

Pisco Sour

4 jiggers pisco
1 jigger fresh lemon juice
Sugar to taste

1 teaspoon egg white (optional)
Ice cubes

Combine the ingredients in a cocktail shaker, shake vigorously with ice cubes, then strain into a glass. Larger amounts may be made by stirring the pisco and lemon juice in a jug with plenty of ice. This is a fairly potent drink and it may satisfactorily be made with equal parts of pisco and lemon juice.

Pisco Collins

2 jiggers pisco
1 jigger fresh lemon juice
Ice cubes

1 teaspoon sugar
Mineral or tonic water

Pour the ingredients into a tumbler and stir with the ice.

Pisco Orange

1 jigger pisco
1 jigger fresh orange juice
2 jiggers dry white wine

Sugar to taste
Ice cubes

Stir well in a jug with abundant ice cubes and strain into a glass.

Chilean Manhattan

2 jiggers pisco
1 jigger vermouth, sweet or dry
to taste

Few drops of Angostura bitters
Ice cubes

Engraving of traditional
pisco still

Stir well with ice cubes and strain into a cocktail glass. Decorate with
a maraschino cherry.

Michael Jackson has remarked in his *Cocktail and Bar Book* (Mitchell
Beazley, 1983), that pisco is 'perhaps the next modish spirit, inexorable
as the fashions of drinking now are', so that the field for experimenta-
tion is wide open!

FORTIFIED WINES

The fortified wines are of minor importance.

Pajarete
This is made in the III and IV Regions from the approved types of
grape (*see p.163*) by adding alcohol to the must during fermentation,
so raising the strength to some 16 per cent by volume. It is then
matured for eighteen to twenty months in raulí. Pale yellow in colour,
it is sweet and somewhat maderized without any marked taste of fruit.

Vino Asoleado
As the name implies, this is a sweet dessert wine made in the south
of Chile in the unirrigated area between the Rivers Mataquito and
Bío-Bío from fruit grown in the district and left in the sun to concentrate the sugar content of the grapes. It may be made from either
black or white grapes, and the minimum alcohol content is 14 per
cent by volume. The red wines are sometimes labelled 'tipo Málaga',
but by courtesy only, since they lack the fruit and intensity of the
genuine article.

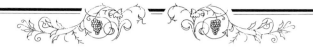

CHAPTER SEVEN

The Producers and
their Wines

The domestic wine market comprises two main sectors: the national
brands and others. Some 65 per cent of sales are of wine made by
small regional wineries or producers, who sell directly, often in 5-litre
carafes. The national brands, made by wineries with a higher level
of technology and embracing the well-known names, account for 35
per cent of the market. It is, in the main, with these that the tasting
notes are concerned.

Of the national brands, the market share at the time of writing
is:

Viña Concha y Toro	24%	
Viñ San Pedro	19%	The Big Four
Viña Santa Rita	28%	
Viña Santa Carolina	10%	
Viña Undurraga	3%	
Others	16%	
	___	
	100%	

We tasted some 250 wines during a month's visit to Chile in November 1984, but it was impossible to taste every good wine made in
Chile or to visit all of its wineries, and we apologize for omissions.
It should be borne in mind that European and Chilean tastes do not
always coincide, so that we have sometimes preferred a younger wine
to an oaky old *reserva*.

Unless otherwise indicated, the wines were tasted in November
1984, and the initials refer to the tasters: *H.J.*, Hugh Johnson; *J.R.*,
Jan Read; *M.R.*, Maite Manjón de Read. Later tastings in the UK of

newer vintages are dated, and our thanks go to Mr Lance Sharpus-Jones (*L. S-J.*) of the Wine Byre in Cupar; to Mr Ian Fenton (*I.F.*) of Peter Dominic, St Andrews; and to Dr Hugh Morris (*H.M.*), who joined us on occasion.

The notes deal first with wines from companies, private or public, and then with cooperative-made wines.

Casona

Controlled by Viña Undurraga (q.v.), this is a small company founded in 1980. It owns no vineyards. The capacity of the bodega is 750,000 litres in wood and 250,000 litres in cement; average annual sales amount to 2,500 cases in the domestic market and 2,500 cases abroad.

Its two labels are:

Gran Vino Blanco (Sauvignon Blanc)
Gran Vino Tinto (Cabernet Sauvignon)

Champagne Alberto Valdivieso SA

Valdivieso, founded in 1879, is the largest producer of sparkling wine in Chile, making it by the original Champagne method.

The company owns 85 hectares of vineyards in the VII Region, centring on Talca. They are planted with:

Pinot Blanc	20 ha
Torontel	20 ha
Chardonnay	15 ha
Cabernet Sauvignon	8 ha
Sauvignon Blanc	6 ha
Sémillon	6 ha

The winery in Santiago has a capacity of 3,500,000 litres in wood, 1,500,000 litres in cement and 150,000 litres in stainless steel. The wines are made by the traditional method of dosing the young wine with sugar and cultivated yeasts, filling it into stout Champagne-type bottles, temporarily corked and left in a cool cellar until such time as the sugar has been converted to carbon dioxide. The bottles are then gradually up-ended in a *pupitre*, so that the fine sediment falls towards the neck of the bottle, which is finally frozen and uncorked, and the plug containing the sediment is forcibly expelled by the pressure of gas inside.

Average domestic sales amount to a sizeable 160,000 cases a year, while 10,000 cases are exported.

Apart from two still wines, a red Cabernet Sauvignon and a white Chardonnay, the labels of the sparkling wines are:

Champagne Chileno Valdivieso
    Gran Brut
    Brut
    Nature
    Gran Demi Sec
    Demi Sec
    Rosé
    Moscato

Sparkling Wine

Champagne Gran Brut NV

Checking bottles of wine for clarity at Viña Canepa

J.R. Very pale straw. Clean, fragrant nose. Clean and fresh, but without a great deal of fruit. Medium mousse, a very enjoyable sparkling wine.

Red Wine

Gran Vino Vieja Cosecha N.V.
J.R. Dark ruby with orange rim. Good Cabernet nose with trace of oiliness, which disappeared on airing. Mellow and fruity with good flavour, body and finish.   *M.T.R.* Round, good balance.

Champagne Subercaseaux

The firm, which is owned by Viña Concha y Toro (q.v.), was founded in 1967 and takes its name from that of the Subercaseaux family (*see p.97*). Don Ramón Subercaseaux Mercado planted the first vineyards at Pirque; and it was his daughter, Doña Emiliana, who with her husband, the Marqués de Casa Concha, founded Viña Concha y Toro.

The wines are made at the Pirque winery of Concha y Toro by the *cuves closes* method (*see p.61*), mostly from Riesling and Sémillon grapes. The pressurized tanks used for the second fermentation, with a total capacity of 120,000 litres, are cooled and thickly lagged, so as to maintain a temperature of 14–16°c. Fermentation normally lasts for four weeks, but the export quality 'Brut' is fermented for six weeks at 10–11°c.

The wines are among the best of their type made in Chile, clean, fresh and with good mousse. There is still a little residual sweetness in the 'Brut', while the 'Demi Sec' and the 'Moscato' – which has a very fragrant Moscatel nose and full varietal flavour – are very definitely on the sweet side.

Average annual sales amount to 47,915 cases in the home market and 479 cases abroad.

José Canepa y Cía Ltda

The firm was founded in 1930 by Don José Canepa Vaccarezza, who was of Italian descent, and it remains a family concern. Since then its wines have won dozens of medals in international exhibitions: in London, Paris, Geneva, Rotterdam, Brussels, Eastern Europe and elsewhere. In 1970, Canepa was awarded a special Gold Medal by the Chilean Wine Exporters Association for outstanding performance in producing and exporting the wines.

The firm is a leading producer and exporter of fruit; its orchards, extending to some 1,087 hectares, grow apples, peaches, oranges, lemons, avocado pears and nuts – to mention only some. It is also one of the few large producers of olive oil in Chile, while its farms and stock-raising establishments provide eggs and beef.

Its vineyards extend to some 600 hectares; those of Caperana and

El Recreo are located in the Maipo Valley near Santiago, and those of Peteroa and San Jorge in the Province of Curicó. All are in the Central Zone. The principal grapes are the white Sémillon and Sauvignon Blanc, and the black Cabernet Sauvignon and Cot. The yield from its own vineyards amounts to about an annual 6,500,000 litres, but according to the demand for the wines, Canepa also buys large amounts of fruit, mostly Cabernet Sauvignon, carefully chosen from the best regions of the country between the provinces of Aconcagua and Talca.

Until 1981, the wines were vinified in a bodega in Valparaiso, which is still used as a warehouse and distribution centre and is particularly useful, since it is near the port.

The large new plant at Maipú, on the outskirts of Santiago, is the most modern in Chile – and possibly in South America. All the wine, both white and red, is vinified in temperature-controlled stainless steel tanks, the whites at 18°c or less, and the reds at 23°c or less. Made in California and heavily ribbed to withstand earthquakes, there are two tanks of 38,500 litres, twenty-seven of 56,200 litres and fourteen of 115,000 litres, all controlled from a central console. In addition, there is a further capacity of 3,041,148 litres for storing the wine in stainless steel. The rest of the equipment is equally up-to-date and culled from the ends of the earth: crushers from Italy; refrigeration equipment from Australia; centrifuges from Germany and a bottling line with an output of 12,000 bottles per hour from Argentina. There are also old wooden vats and casks for maturing the red wines, with a combined capacity of 1,200,000 litres, and space for storing 3 million bottles.

The company has been exporting to Europe, mainly to Belgium, Switzerland and Germany, for thirty-six years and also sells its wines to Japan and almost all the countries of South America.

One of us (H.J.) shipped the 1968 Cabernet Sauvignon in its early days. It was duly bottled in the cellars of Saling Hall, and we can both testify to the quality of that beautiful vintage over the years.

White Wines

Opposite
Hydraulic basket press dating from the 19th century and preserved at Concha y Toro after the installation of modern equipment

Sauvignon Blanc 1985 (tasted 20.12.86)
100% Sauvignon Blanc from Maipo. 12° alcohol.   *J.R.* Pale yellow. Fragrant Sauvignon Blanc flowering currant nose. Very fresh, peachy flavour, plenty of substance, touch of sweetness. Long finish. First rate.

Sauvignon Blanc 1983
H.J. Fairly gold. Fresh nose. Fairly full and definitely fruity style, not

Above
Staking the vines in the vineyards of Concha y Toro at Peumo

Pais vines

grassy. Fairly low acid, but substantial, almost 'luscious' (*J.R.*).   *J.R.* Pale straw. Clean, fragrant nose. Fruity flavour, a little sweet, but not unpleasantly so. Low acidity. Luscious. Nice.   *M.R.* Good, Gentle nose. Full, luscious. Low acidity.

Riesling 1980

Aged for four years in wooden *cubas* of 30,000–40,000 litres.   *H.J.* Bright gold. No wood smell. Soft dry wine with old closet flavour.   *J.R.* Very odd nose and flavour. Camphor. Mothballs, Not attractive.   *M.R.* Wood masquerading as mothballs.

'Finisimo' Sauvignon Blanc 1980

Aged for four years in wood.   *H.J.* Soft, dry, good flavours. Totally clean and unoxidized. Not thrilling, but very sound.   *J.R.* Nice clean fruity nose. Straightforward drinking wine. Not oxidized. Very pleasant.   *M.R.* Attractive, fresh and long.

Red Wines

Cabernet Sauvignon 1984 (from the tank)

From the firm's Curicó vineyards. 12.7° alcohol.   *H.J.* Splendid colour. Very good Cabernet Sauvignon nose. Slightly grassy, ripe. Big, sweet, juicy, excellent. Bloody good.   *J.R.* Young, dark plum colour. Yeasty nose. Lots of fruit – blackberries etc. Sweet. Excellent.   *M.R.* Lovely Ribena colour. Very attractive and good.

Cabernet Sauvignon 1980

Three years in wood.   *H.J.* Mature colour. Delicious mature nose. Clean and fruity, but over-aged.   *J.R.* Ruby with orange rim. Nice Cabernet + wood nose. Medium weight and fruit. Very ripe for an '80. Pleasant – but not for laying down.   *M.R.* Attractive nose, oak plus fruit. A bit dry and has seen better days.

'Finisimo' Cabernet Sauvignon 1977

Six years in wood.   *H.J.* Much darker colour. Oaky old smell with traces of resin and sweetness. Too tired.   *J.R.* Dark ruby with orange rim. Very pronounced oaky nose. Not much fruit. Has lost body, finishes oaky without fruit.   *M.R.* Rich orange colour, but too oaky. Intense taste of wood. Not pleasing.

Cabernet Sauvignon 1976

Five years in wood and four in bottle.   *H.J.* Very dark. Slightly unclean nose. Fruit disintegrated. Much too old.   *J.R.* Very dense colour. Overripe, raisin nose. Slightly oily. Oxidized, gone alto-gether. *M.R.* More aromatic than the one before, but going to the grave.

Cabernet Sauvignon 1968

Harvested in a drought year and bottled as 'Finisimo' in '72. The wine was made for export to Cuba and bottled for Fidel Castro. *H.J.* Very dark. Very oaky, but still good *roasted* fruit. Huge old wine on its last legs. Super. *J.R.* Mahogany colour, a little turbid. Old Cabernet Sauvignon flavour. The remains of a remarkable wine. *M.R.* Per-fumed oaky nose. Full-bodied and oaky. Over the peak, but in good shape for its age.

Miguel Torres (Chile) Ltda

The firm of Torres, with headquarters in Vilafranca del Penedès near Barcelona, is among the most respected in Spain and one of the largest exporters of Spanish wines, especially to the USA. Seeking to expand its activities in 1978 it acquired the small bodegas of Viña Maquehua near Curicó, the property of the Ahrex family since 1904, together with 100 hectares of vineyards.

By 1979 it was energetically replanting the vineyards and had embarked on the complete modernization of the winery. Stainless steel fermentation tanks were brought from Catalonia; large numbers of new 300-litre American oak *barricas* were installed for maturing the red wines, together with a battery of new equipment, including Vaslin horizontal presses, refrigeration plant and up-to-date filtration devices.

The entry of Torres into the Chilean wine industry was much more than the arrival on the scene of a foreign firm. Miguel A. Torres is one of the world's most accomplished winemakers and for the first time in Chile he set about making white wines by 'cold fermentation', so exploiting the remarkable quality of the fruit to the full. The new white wines were immediately successful in foreign markets, and other enlightened Chilean wine firms were quick to consult with him and to follow his example. What has recently set the seal on his achieve-ment has been the award, in competition with wines from all over the world, of no less than one gold and two silver medals for Torres red, white and rosé wines from Chile at the 1985 Olympia Wine Fair in London, together with a special award for 'exceptional wine-making'.

Some 50 hectares of the vineyards, planted with Cabernet Sauvignon and Sauvignon Blanc, are now in full production, and a further 100 hectares are currently being planted with Riesling, Gewürztraminer and Chardonnay. In addition, the firm buys very carefully selected Cabernet Sauvignon, Riesling, Chardonnay and Gewürztraminer from areas in which they are grown to the best advantage.

Total capacity in 1986 amounted to 750,000 litres in stainless steel and 283,500 litres in 300-litre *barricas* of new American oak, but is being continuously expanded. Exports, mainly to the USA, stood at 22,629 cases.

White Wines

'Santa Digna' Sauvignon Blanc 1986 (tasted 19.12.86)
J.R. Very pale straw with greenish cast. Delicately fragrant nose — passion fruit, lichees. Dry, light, fruity and refreshing. Very slight pétillance. Longish fruit finish. Very good. Left overnight in a corked bottle, it retained all of its nose and the flavour was rather fuller and peachier. M.R. Palest bright yellow. Minty, gooseberry nose, delicately aromatic. Slight pétillance. Dry and refreshing. Longish smoky finish. Very good.

'Don Miguel' Riesling 1986 (tasted 18.12.86)
J.R. Pale yellow. Delicate, flowery Riesling nose. Full Riesling flavour, touch of sweetness. Perhaps a little thin and a shade short at the finish. M.R. Pale yellow, bright, pretty colour. Good Riesling nose. Fresh, clean, but very light and the finish somewhat short.

'Bellaterra' Sauvignon Blanc 1985 (tasted 4.12.86)
Sauvignon Blanc with four months in oak *barrica*. M.R. Pale yellow with greenish cast. Peachy nose. Buttery, elegant, lovely mixture of peaches and gentle oak with a hint of herbs in the middle. Lingering finish, but lightweight compared with the 1983. J.R. Fragrant peachy nose. and flavour. Light, a little oaky. Nice, but lacks the intensity of the 1983.

'Bellaterra' Sauvignon Blanc 1983
H.J. Pretty gold. Peachy smell, nice toasty oak. A bit over-oaked but attractive. J.R. Good nose. Full flavour with some oak. Peachy. Very nice. M.R. Peachy nose. Flavour follows, and it is *lovely*.
(tasted 27.9.85)
J.R. Pale lemon yellow. Full, fruity, peachy nose — almost Chardonnay (but, in fact, Sauvignon Blanc). Full-bodied, full of flavour, long finish. Wonderful. (Several days after opening, the wine, when kept in the door of the fridge, retained practically all of its beautiful nose and flavour.)

Rosé Wine

'Santa Digna Rosé' 1986 (tasted 31.8.86)
J.R. Pretty, light cherry colour. Elegant fruity fragrance. Delicate, dry. Very fresh, but a little light? Very nice.   *M.R.* Pretty pink colour, brilliant. Very fruity nose. Fragrant, elegant. Slightly smoky taste, long finish.   *L. S.-J.* Pink deep/onion skin. Light fragrant nose (hint of cigar-box). Round ripe apricot taste, dry finish, not distinctive but pleasant. Earthy hint.

'Santa Digna Rosé' 1983 (tasted 18.9.85)
J.R. Attractive pale-brown-orange colour. Delicate fruity nose. Light, delicate fruit – strawberries. Some complexity. Good finish. Dry, light and delightful.

Red Wines

'Santa Digna' Cabernet Sauvignon 1984 (tasted 31.8.86)
H.J. Fairly pale red, even colour. Nose backward. Very clean tannic impact, fresh clean fruit flavours without great depth/sweetness. Very long and promising finish, elegant and convincing.   *J.R.* Ruby. Good light Cabernet nose. Round, fruity and fairly tannic. Raspberry flavour. Lightish wine, but with long finish. Should improve in bottle. Nice.

'Santa Digna' Cabernet Sauvignon 1983
Aged for fifteen months in 300-litre *barricas*.   *H.J.* Strong Cabernet nose. Rather pale. Slightly green: Monterey style. Light and pleasant, grassy.   *J.R.* Ruby. Fresh plummy nose. Light Cabernet Sauvignon flavour. Very fresh, but a little short.

'Santa Digna' Cabernet Sauvignon 1982
H.J. Darker, but not very dark. Cabernet Sauvignon + oak, slightly inky. Lightish weight. More guts than the '83, just. But slightly volatile (ditto oak).
  (tasted Dec. 1986)
H.J. Mid-deep red, unfaded. Fresh herby Cabernet France-style nose and light flavours. Still youthful and lively, good balance, but not quite as full and not quite as long in the finish as '84.

'Santa Digna' Cabernet Sauvignon 1981 (tasted 11.11.85)
Two years in American oak and remainder in bottle.   *J.R.* Clear orange-ruby. Clean fruity Cabernet Sauvignon nose. Light, but very good fruity flavour. Well-balanced, long finish. Excellent.

Sociedad Agrícola Santa Elisa Ltda

One of the newer firms, Santa Elisa was founded in 1978. It owns 281 hectares of vineyards in the VI Region, planted with:

Cabernet Sauvignon	174 ha
Cot (or Malbec)	69 ha
Sémillon	23 ha
Chardonnay	13 ha
Pinot Noir	2 ha

The vinification plant at Chimbarango, just south of San Fernando, has a capacity of 1,797,000 litres in wood and 206,000 litres in cement.

Its labels are:

White wine
Sauvignon: Reserva Especial (Sauvignon Blanc)
Rosé wine
Rosé Reserva Especial (Merlot)
Red wine
Cabernet Sauvignon: Reserva Especial

Sociedad Viña Carmen

Founded in 1850, the firm now belongs to Viña Canepa (q.v.). It owns 113 hectares in the Maipo Valley, planted with:

Sauvignon Blanc	44 ha
Cabernet Sauvignon	36 ha
Cot (or Malbec)	14 ha
Riesling	12 ha
Pinot Noir	7 ha

The winery at Buin, south of Santiago, has a capacity of 1,400,000 litres in wooden receptacles of different sizes.

Its labels are:

White wines
'Rhin Reserva de Oro'
'Gran Vino Rhin Carmen'
Pinot Blanc
'Gran Vino'
Red wines
'Margaux Reserva de Oro'
'Gran Vino Carmen Margaux'
Pinot Noir
'Gran Vino'

Urmeneta

José Tomas Urmeneta was a wealthy owner of silver mines in the north of Chile and, following the example of his son-in-law, Silvestre Ochagavía, was one of the first to plant noble French vines in Chile. Together with those of Ochagavía and Errásuriz-Panquehue, the Urmeneta wines were the best-known in Chile at the period of the early French plantations from 1851 onwards. They now exist in name only and are made by Viña San Pedro (q.v.) for export to the USA (but are not sold in Chile itself).

The labels are:

White wine
Urmeneta Sauvignon Blanc
Rosé wine
Urmeneta Rosé
Red wine
Urmeneta Cabernet

Viña Concha y Toro SA

Concha y Toro is the largest of the Chilean wine companies, and with foreign sales running at some 300,000 cases annually, one of the few to have made a sizeable impact in export markets.

The story begins with Don Ramón Subercaseaux Mercado, who had made an immense fortune from his silver mines in northern Chile. Towards the middle of the nineteenth century Don Ramón bought the large estate of Pirque on the outskirts of Santiago. At the time, the land was dry and arid, but by constructing an irrigation canal and diverting waters from the River Maipo, he was able to transform it into good agricultural land. He next bought a farm, still known as the Chacra Subercaseaux, and engaged an experienced French wine-maker, a M. Bachelet, to plant a vineyard. At the same time, a bodega and houses for the workers were built on the site, now belonging to Concha y Toro. Over the following years, more French vines were planted and the bodegas were extended, so that the little farmstead became the nucleus of a growing industry, and Don Ramón's son was able to proclaim in his autobiography, *Memorias de ochenta años*: 'Here was made the first wine in the French style.'

Don Ramón's daughter, Doña Emiliana, who is commemorated today in the name of a range of wines, had meanwhile married a brilliant young politician and businessman, the aristocratic Don Melchor de Concha y Toro, the Marqués de Casa Concha. On Don Ramón's death, the two threw themselves wholeheartedly into the further expansion of the winery, and Don Melchor engaged another French oenologist, the talented M. de Labouchère, who brought with him a selection of the best French vines, which were planted in the Pirque vineyards.

In 1883, the firm was established under the name of Viña Concha y Toro. On the advice of Labouchère, Don Melchor subsequently acquired an estate at Cachapoal near Rancagua. Its vineyards, together with those at Pirque, are today the largest belonging to Concha y Toro. Extensive works were also carried out at Pirque in building a new bodega, in equipping it with casks of Bosnian and American oak and in constructing underground cellars for the bottle-ageing of the wines.

After the death of Don Melchor in 1892, his widow, Doña Emiliana, continued his work, and it was on her initiative that Concha y Toro became a public company in 1923. At the same time it bought the rights to the labels of the Subercaseaux wines, and the name survives in the sparkling wines made by Concha y Toro since 1967. The famous premium quality 'Casillero del Diablo' was first marketed in 1963; the company's choicest *reserva*, the 'Marqués de Casa Concha', is named in honour of Don Melchor.

Entrance to the Pirque bodegas of Viña Concha y Toro

97

Although the family sold out its shareholdings in 1923, it is still involved with the firm. The son of the present Marqués de Casa Concha, Chilean ambassador to Norway, is a director, as is Don Fernando Adunate Errázuriz, who is married to Doña Sofía Concha. Control now lies with the energetic General Manager and Director, Don Alfonso Larraín Santa María, and his brother Don Andrés, who is in charge of viticulture and vineyards. The chief oenologist, Sr Goetz von Gersdorff von Goetz, joined the firm from Germany twenty years ago and has done much to improve the quality of the white wines.

Concha y Toro owns in all 1,391 hectares of vineyards, in production or planted. They are located at Pirque and Maipo in the Maipo Valley; at Viluco, near Buin; at Cachapoal, west of Rancagua; at Totihue, near Requinoa; at La Gloria and Las Palmeras, west of San Fernando; and at El Estero, north of Curicó. The largest holding is at Cachapoal. At the time of the Revolution in 1970, the company owned only 100 hectares of vineyards in this area, but has subsequently bought up some 3,000 hectares of land, most of which will eventually be planted with vines or fruit trees. It employs some 600 workers on the estate, which embraces a large bodega with a capacity of $8\frac{1}{2}$ million litres, houses for the employees and a floodlit football pitch – the firm mounts its own team.

At the time of writing, Concha y Toro's vineyards are planted with different vine varieties as follows:

Cabernet Sauvignon	769 ha
Merlot	168 ha
Sémillon	106 ha
Riesling	92 ha
Cot (Malbec)	74 ha
Sauvignon Blanc	73 ha
Chardonnay	66 ha
Verdot	28 ha
Gewürztraminer	9 ha
Chenin Blanc	6 ha

To maintain the large output, grapes are also bought from independent farmers.

Apart from the main bodega at Pirque, the firm also owns vinification plants at San Miguel (on the site of the Chacra Subercaseaux), Maipo, Buin, Cachapoal, La Gloria, Las Palmeras, El Estero, Pedehue and Lontué – its tankers ferrying wine from the outlying bodegas to the main winery at Pirque are a common sight on the Pan American Highway. The white wines are now fermented at 13–18°c at the Maipo winery, which is equipped with eleven temperature-controlled stainless steel tanks, each of 100,000 litres capacity, imported from

Catalonia. Between them, the total capacity of the plants amounts to 22,962,000 litres in wood, 28,268,000 litres in epoxy-coated cement vats and 1,100,000 litres in stainless steel tanks.

The old winery at Pirque is one of the most picturesque in Chile. Through a lofty gateway with a tiled pediment and the name 'Concha y Toro' writ large in wrought iron, one enters a small paradise of flowering trees, beds of brilliant red geranium, colonnaded patios and, of course, the old bodega itself, in whose cool reaches the old oak and raulí casks vanish into the dark. Visitors are welcome, and the tour, conducted by a willowy hostess with raven-black hair and a flashing smile, ends in an elegant tasting room and a cooling glass of Subercaseaux *champagna* – and whatever else takes one's fancy.

.. Over the last three years, domestic sales of the wines have averaged a hefty 2,896,373 cases, with 409,195 cases going for export; under its efficient management, Concha y Toro is one of the Chilean wine firms to turn in consistently large profits.

The Peumo bodega of Concha y Toro

99

White Wines

'Santa Emiliana' Sauvignon Blanc 1983 (Domestic market)
From Maipo. Four to six months in 2,000-litre oak *fudres*, 12.6° alcohol, total acidity 5.2 g/litre.　*H.J.* Very slightly woody nose, faint wood flavour giving a bit of substance, but dry finish.　*J.R.* Pale straw. Not very much nose. Faint oak and some fruit. Dry finish. Pleasant.

Sauvignon Blanc 1984 (Export)
From Maipo. 13° alcohol, total acidity 5.2 g/litre, pH 3.4, 2–2.5 g/litre residual sugar. Made in stainless steel and bottled at five months.　*H.J.* Slight Sauvignon Blanc nose. Very pleasantly fruity with slight sweetness.　*J.R.* Pronounced fruity nose, more so than the first. Much fruitier taste, with longer, less dry finish.

Sauvignon Blanc – Sémillon 1984 (Export, magnum bottle)
10% Sauvignon and 90% Sémillon from Maipo. 2–2.5 g/litre residual sugar. Just bottled.　*H.J.* Slightly less Sauvignon Blanc nose, but equal flavour. Harsher. Needs bottle age.　*J.R.* Pale straw. Not a great deal of nose. Slight fragrance, but needs bottle age.

'Santa Emiliana' Chardonnay 1983 (Domestic and Export)
From Totihue. No malolactic fermentation, clarified immediately after fermentation with addition of SO_2. 12.6° alcohol, pH 3.3.　*H.J.* Lemon colour, slight bubble. Very good Chardonnay nose. Slightly prickly/harsh and a bit short.　*J.R.* Pale straw. Good Chardonnay nose. Somewhat neutral in taste and finish a bit short. Lacks roundness and freshness. Pleasant, but a bit bland.

Chardonnay 1982 (Export)
From Totihue. Two years in bottle, the first wine to be cold fermented in stainless steel.　*H.J.* Clean Chardonnay nose. Two years bottle age just shows in richer nose. More flavour, punchy middle and length. Trace of bitterness? Not much finesse, but a good dry Chardonnay.　*J.R.* Rather deeper in colour and nose, but a bit sharp and lacking body and roundness.

'Oro del Rhin' Riesling-Sauvignon 1983 (Domestic and Export)
From Maipo. Contains 5% Moscatel and has some age in red Chilean or American oak. 12° alcohol, pH 3.3 residual sugar 16 g/litre.　*H.J.* Slight muscat nose. Rather catty and harsh flavour. Not too sweet – the whites are, in general, a bit timid.　*J.R.* Muscat nose. Not particularly sweet. A bit of a hotch-potch.

Rosé Wine

'Santa Emiliana' Merlot Rosé 1984

From Cachapoal. Residual sugar 14 g/litre.　*H.J.* Vin d'une nuit. Fading cherry. Good fresh fruity nose, a little bland, but round and a little velouté.　*J.R.* Light cherry colour. Very fresh fruity nose. Sweeter than the others. Smooth, fruity, easy to drink.

Red Wines

Cabernet Sauvignon 1984 (future 'Casillero del Diablo')

From Pirque. At present in 20,000-litre raulí *cubas*, will then have one-and-a-half to two years maximum in 2,000-litre casks. The contents of the different casks will be blended and clarified before bottling in 1987. Grapes late-harvested in April. 13.5° alcohol, total acidity 4.5 g/litre, pH 3.6. Low yield of 4–5 tonnes/ha.　*H.J.* Deep mulberry colour. Good ripe (not very) Cabernet Sauvignon nose. Concentrated, clean, big tannic husky, slightly inky – not very fruity.　*J.R.* Very dark, impenetrable inky colour. Young plummy nose. Good blackberry flavour.　*M.R.* Marvellous fruity nose, plummy, vinous. Gutsy and good. Long.

Cabernet Sauvignon – Merlot 1982 (Export in magnums)

From Cachapoal and Rapel Valley. 25% Merlot. Yield 15 tonnes/ha. Will spend two years in 20,000-litre raulí *cubas* and be bottled this year.　*H.J.* Lighter colour and nose. More nip, nice tangy cut. Fairly shallow, but attractive. High yield lightness.　*J.R.* Dark cherry. Nice, but not very pronounced nose. Fresh, fruity. Attractive, quite tannic. Brisk.　*M.R.* Good, gutsy.

Cabernet Sauvignon 1981 (Export)
'Santa Emiliana' (Domestic)

Selected Cabernet Sauvignon from Maipo and Cachapoal. One year in 20,000-litre *cubas* and one in 2,000-litre casks. To be bottled this year. Sells 3 million litres yearly. 12.4° alcohol, total acidity 4.8 g/litre, pH 3.6.　*H.J.* Attractive fruit/berry nose. Dark mid-red. Some richness, nice and brisky and brambly. Very good.　*J.R.* Dark cherry. Good Cabernet Sauvignon nose. Excellent fruity Cabernet flavour. Good balance, not too heavy (costs 70 pesos in local markets!).　*M.R.* Good colour, round, long finish.

'Casillero del Diablo' 1980 (Export and Domestic)

From Pirque. Harvested in April. One-and-a-half years in 2,000-litre casks, one year in bottle. 12.5° alcohol, total acidity 5 g/litre, pH 3.5.   *H.J.* Richer nose. Colour shows maturity. Some berry sweetness- + distinct oak on the nose. Astringent at end. Enough velvet?   *J.R.* Deep ruby with orange rim. Pronounced oaky nose. Soft, deep, beautiful. Oak + blackcurrants. Long finish.   *M.R.* Bright colour and Cabernet Sauvignon nose. Fruity, round, long finish. Very good.

'Casillero del Diablo' 1978 Reserva

100% Cabernet Sauvignon from Pirque. Bottled November 1981.   *H.J.* Colour showing maturity. Mercaptan nose and brimstone flavour right through to dried-up end. Disappointing.   *J.R.* Dark ruby with orange rim. Very oaky, but the fruit is unclean and spoilt by mercaptan (organic sulphur), which is very evident at the finish.   *M.R.* Bright orange. Mercaptan in nose. Wine follows. Not a good finish.

'Casillero del Diablo' 1977

100% Cabernet Sauvignon from Pirque. Bottled in 1981.   *H.J.* Similar + rather mulberry richness. Only faint sulphur problems at finish. Oak nicely blended with fruit. Total effect slightly fleeting.   *J.R.* Richer, fuller. Oak + fruit. Still a little mercaptan at end, but a lovely wine.   *M.R.* A little mercaptan. Blackberry tase and full complex wine. Very good.

'Santa Emiliana' Cabernet Sauvignon 1976

From Maipo and Cachapoal. Five to six years in bottle. Bristol Double Gold Award 1980.   *H.J.* Full mature red. Gentle, ripe but unassertive nose. Round wine, easy character, a shade simple in maturity.   *J.R.* Dark ruby, orange rim. Oak-mercaptan. Sweetish edge to it, but over the peak. Has been very nice.   M.R. Bright rusty colour. Cabernet Sauvignon nose, wet leaves. Round, but must be drunk soon.

'Marqués de Casa Concha' 1984

100% Cabernet Sauvignon from San José.   *H.J.* Beautiful colour, still inky. High acid, prickly with malolactic. Deep and round.

'Marques de Casa Concha' 1983

H.J. Quite broad. Good flavour. Tannic; a bit blunt and short at present.

'Marques de Casa Concha' 1982

H.J. Nose turning sweet with wood. Rich and complex. Tannic, rather hard. Covered depth – big dry finish.

'Marques de Casa Concha' Gran Vino 1980
100% Cabernet Sauvignon from Puerto Alto, Maipo Valley. One year in a large wooden *cubas*, two years in casks, one year in bottle. (Oenologist commented that four years was ideal for Chilean Cabernet.) *J.R.* Good Cabernet Sauvignon nose. Round, smooth, soft, good body. Long Cabernet finish. Excellent.   *M.R.* Fruity and wood in nose, orange rim and lovely concentrated nose and finish. Elegant, a perfect wine.

'Marqués de Casa Concha' 1978
M.R. Bright ruby-orange. Good fruity bouquet. Oaky flavour with lots of fruit. Round, long finish. Excellent.

'Marqués de Casa Concha' 1975
M.R. Bright orange colour. Nose oaky rather than fruity. A bit maderized and finish a little dry.

'Conde de la Conquista' 1983
75% Cabernet Sauvignon and 25% Merlot from Peumo.   *M.R.* Plummy nose, fresh, pleasant, but short.

Viña Cousiño Macul – Arturo Cousiño Lyon

The vineyards of Macul, on the outskirts of Santiago, are the oldest in Chile. The lands were granted to Juan Jufré, one of the lieutenants of the Conquistador Pedro de Valdivia, in 1546; and it is on record that they had been planted with vines by 1554. The area had earlier been colonized by Mitimae Indians, who came with Incas from Peru and named it 'Macul' in memory of a village of the same name in their homeland. In Quechua, the language of the Incas, 'Macul' means 'right hand'.

Over the years, the estate changed hands at intervals, finally passing to the present owners, the Cousiño family, during the latter part of the nineteenth century. About 1870 Don Luis Cousiño rooted up the País vines, replanting the vineyards with noble varieties brought from France, including the Cabernet Sauvignon, Riesling and Sauvignon Blanc, and constructing a bogeda in French style to vinify them.

The family was one of the wealthiest in Chile; Don Luis owned coal mines in the south – during the war with Peru of 1879–83, he provided coal free of charge to the government – and his wife, Doña Isadora, silver mines at Copiapó in the north. Apart from the estate at Macul, which, in addition to the winery and vineyards, embraces a beautiful house and a large park landscaped in English style, the monumental and spendidly decorated Palacio Cousiño in Santiago,

built by Doña Isadora after her husband's death, was at the beginning
of the century used for distributing the wines in the capital. Bottled
at the winery, they were taken to cellars in the Palace, from which
orders were supplied. Sold to the Municipality of Santiago in 1941,
it has more recently been used as an official residence for visiting
heads of state, such as Marshal Tito, President de Gaulle and Golda
Meir.

Near Concepción the family laid out another famous park at Lota,
very different in style from that at Macul. It was planned by the same
English landscape gardener, but is semi-tropical and occupies a pre-
cipitous peninsula, flanked on either side by the mines and jetties of
the Cousiño mining company. In the mining town of Lota itself,
schools, hospitals and institutes all bear the names of different genera-
tions of the Cousiños: Don Luis, Doña Isadora, Don Matías and the
rest.

Cousiño Macul is still a family company, its present head being
Don Arturo Cousiño Lyon, whose son Don Carlos is also actively
involved.

It is one of the few in Chile to grow all of its own fruit. The 264
hectares, directly adjoining the winery and park, lie in the Maipo Valley with the foothills of the Andes rising abruptly behind them. The
distribution of vine varieties is:

White
Sémillon   31.99 ha
Sauvignon Blanc   23.04 ha
Riesling   18.20 ha
Chardonnay   14.61 ha

Black
Cabernet Sauvignon   175.66 ha
Merlot   5.11 ha

The vines are grown in the firm's own nurseries and transplanted after
the first year, yielding a small crop in the fourth. Average annual yield
is 2,850,000 litres.

The first bodegas were built about 1870 by a French architect and
incorporated spacious arched cellars at 6 metres below ground level,
where the temperature varies by only 1°c over the year, so providing
the optimum environment for the maturation of the wines. With
modern additions, the storage capacity amounts to 2,620,000 litres
in cement vats and 5,430,000 litres in wood, mostly American oak.
There is further capacity for ageing 1,200,000 bottles of wine.

The white wines are vinified at low temperatures for some fifteen days, so as to conserve the bouquet and fruit, and the red for four to five days in normal fashion.

Cousiño Macul is a name to conjure with in Chile, and its wines, especially the Cabernet Sauvignon *reservas*, are among the best-known abroad.

White Wines

'Don Luis' Sauvignon Blanc 1982
The wine was pale yellow and had spent three to four months in raulí casks. *H.J.* Very dry, slight varietal character and slight wood. Old style and a little oxidized. *J.R.* Fragrant nose. Nice balance of fruit and wood. Very dry. Pleasant. *M.R.* Nice blend of wood and fruit in the nose.

'Doña Isadora' Riesling 1982
H.J. No nose, too dry, higher acid. Somewhat dull, but slightly fruity and pleasant enough. *J.R.* Not much nose. Very dry finish with some wood. Very little Riesling character. Too dry. *M.R.* Some wood in the nose. Too dry and not very fragrant or fruity.

Chardonnay 1985 (tasted 15.11.86)
J.R. Brilliant pale straw. Elegant honied Chardonnay nose (*M.R.* 'honeysuckle'). Intense fruity flavour. Almost semi-sweet in the mouth, but dry at finish. An excellent young Chardonnay, very fresh and intense. Gorgeous.

Chardonnay 1983
There was general agreement that of the whites tasted at the bodega this was the most attractive. *H.J.* Good full fruit. Clean, good balance and some length, and very much a Chardonnay. *J.R.* Very pale straw colour. Light, flowery, elegant nose. Good blend of fruit and wood. Good finish, very nice. *M.R.* Pale colour, fruity, nice nose and restrained wood.

Red Wines

Cabernet Sauvignon 1982 (tasted 21.11.86)
J.R. Deep ruby. Nice fruit + oak nose. Dry, soft, good fruit and balance, long finish. Very pleasing.

'Don Luis' Cabernet Sauvignon 1981

Aged in 1,000-litre casks, the wine was ruby-coloured with an orange rim. *H.J.* Grassy Cabernet. Not too woody. Dry, clean and fine. *J.R.* Nice young nose. Very good Cabernet Sauvignon flavour with some oak. Some astringency at the end. Good. *M.R.* Intense blackberry nose. A fresh and individual wine with grip and guts and long finish. Good.

'Don Matías' 1981

Another Cabernet Sauvignon, this was much darker in colour and more full-bodied than the 'Don Luis' of the same year (*M.R.*) ' a big, big wine'. *H.J.* Strong dry tannic, astringent, press wine, mouth-cleaning. A keeper. At dinner in hotel, sweet finish; super. Would go well with lamb. *J.R.* Fruity aromatic (cedarwood?) nose. Young, fruity taste. Plenty of tannin. Should age well.

'Antiguas Reservas' 1977

This is made with Cabernet Sauvignon grapes grown on slopes with maximum exposure to the sun and is aged for three years in casks of American oak and two years in bottle. *H.J.* Good bottle bouquet. No off-tastes. Astringent finish. *J.R.* Brick-red with orange rim. Ripe, fruity nose. Soft fruit with some wood. Somewhat astringent finish. *M.R.* Mellow nose, good fruit and a bit of wood. Good long finish.

Viña Errázuriz-Panquehue Ltda

Viña Panquehue is the only large winery to be situated in the wide Aconcagua Valley. Some 200 km north of Santiago, it is watered by the Aconcagua river descending from the highest peak in the Andes and is cooled by breezes from the Pacific. Although its soils are deep, calcareous and permeable, and ideal for viticulture, they are almost entirely given over to the more profitable dessert grapes.

When Don Maximiano Errázuriz Valdivieso, a member of an old Chilean family of Basque origin, bought a tract in 1870, it was generally believed that his venture was doomed to failure, but by irrigating the apparently barren land and planting it with noble vines from France, he soon created a fertile vineyard. He was a man imbued with a love for vines and once said: 'Grapevines should be carefully tended and treated like a work of art, since their life-span runs parallel to that of man. . . . A vine should be cared for and properly pruned and trained so that its branches bear the highest quality of fruit.'

Don Maximiano had four children by his first wife, Doña Amalia Urmeneta, and both the love of wine-growing and that of art passed

Opposite

Wine tasting: Chile is best known for its Cabernet Sauvignon but is now producing crisp and fruity young white wines

from one generation to the next. While one of his sons, José Tomas, became a noteworthy painter in England, another, Rafael Errázuriz Urmeneta, inherited his father's passion and extended the plantations, so that, with 1,000 hectares, it became the largest single vineyard in the world at the time.

The family of the present owners, the Chadwick family from England, first settled in Chile in 1839; and the mother of J. Alfonso Chadwick, now President of the company, was an Errázuriz, so that there is an unbroken family chain.

Apart from 80 hectares of Cabernet Sauvignon in the Aconcagua Valley, Panquehue owns another 70 hectares planted with Sauvignon Blanc, Sémillon and Chardonnay in the Mataquito Valley in the VII Region far to the south.

The bodega is a picturesque old building on the fringe of the vineyards in the Aconcagua Valley, low-built with tiled roof, with deep underground cellars, where the temperature remains constant at 12°c for maturing the wines. It is equipped with vats and casks of American and Bosnian oak with a total capacity of 2,800,000 litres and concrete vats of another 3,700,000 litres. All the wine is made from grapes grown in the firm's own vineyards.

White Wines

Sauvignon Blanc 1985 (tasted at Vinexpo, Bordeaux, 17.6.85)
M.R. Amost water-white. Marvellously fresh and fragrant generic nose. Light and intensely fruity flavour. Good finish. (J.R. The new-style Chilean whites should be drunk as young as possible, preferably during the year of vintage. Another sample of this same wine tasted on 28.11.86, though clean and refreshing, was left only with a faintly flowery nose, a slight lemony flavour and little finish.)

Sauvignon Blanc 1984
100% Sauvignon Blanc from the Mataquito Valley. Clarified and requiring one further filtration before bottling. 13.4° alcohol, total acidity 3.65 g/litre, residual sugar 1.79 g/litre. J.R. Pale greenish-yellow. Flowery nose. Good fruity flavour and fresh. Sugar a bit low. Nice. M.R. Nice fruity nose. I would like a bit more sugar. Finish rather too dry.

White 'Corton'. Gran Vino 1982
50% Sauvignon Blanc, 50% Sémillon. Matured in epoxy-lined cement vats with six months in American oak *barricas*. 12.8° alcohol, total acidity 3.43 g/litre, residual sugar 4.24 g/litre. J.R. Yellow. Oaky

Opposite top
The famous vineyards of Cousiño Macul at Macul

Opposite bottom
Old bodega at Undurraga

109

nose, no fruit. Very dry. Oaky finish.   *M.R.* Darker colour. Practically no nose. Oaky all the way.

'Doña Leonora'. Antigua Reserva 1980

A special reserve made with 60% Sémillon and 40% Sauvignon Blanc from the Mataquito Valley. 13.2° alcohol, total acidity 3.48 g/litre, residual sugar 5 g/litre. One-and-a-half years in American oak *barricas* and two years in bottle.   *J.R.* Pale yellow. Not much nose, mostly oak. More fruit in the wine, longer finish.   *M.R.* Pale yellow. More fruit in nose and rounder. Long finish. Nice.

Red Wines

Cabernet Sauvignon 1984

100% Cabernet Sauvignon from Aconcagua. In oak for six months. 13.7° alcohol, 3.43 g/litre acidity, residual sugar 1.8 g/litre.   *J.R.* Dark ruby-plum. Lovely blackberry nose. Deep blackcurrant flavour. Fruit all the way.   *M.R.* Plummy colour. Blackberry nose. Round, brisk, long finish. Wonderful.

'Corton' Gran Vino 1982

100% Cabernet Sauvignon from the Aconcagua Valley. Aged for two years in American oak *barricas* at 12°c and one in bottle. 12.4° alcohol, 3.68 g/litre total acidity, 1.7 g/litre residual sugar.   *J.R.* Brick-red. Nice Cabernet Sauvignon nose. Fresh, light, good fruit.   *M.R.* Ripe nose, round and fruity finish.

Gran Vino 1981

60% Cabernet Sauvignon from the Aconcagua Valley and 40% from

Opposite top
The bodegas of Viña Panquehue

Opposite bottom
A vineyard of Viña Panquehue in the Aconcagua Valley

In the cellars of Viña Errazuriz-Panquehue

Curicó. 12.2° alcohol. Six months in oak.   *J.R.* Light cherry colour. Fruity young nose reminiscent of Beaujolais Nouveau. Light, refreshing, good fruit. Marvellous value at its give-away price.   *M.R.* Light plum colour. Beaujolais Nouveau nose. Good fruity flavour and finish. Very pleasant.

'Don Maximiano' 1981
A special reserve made with 100% Cabernet Sauvignon grown in the Aconcagua Valley on the slopes exposed to the sun, with a maximum yield of 4,000 kg/acre. Aged at 12°c for three years in vats of American and Bosnian oak and for two in bottle. 12.2° alcohol, total acidity 3.28 g/litre, residual sugar 1.68 g/litre.   *J.R* Ruby orange. Lighter nose. Good fruit and finish. Very dry. Light, but very fruity. Very nice.   *M.R.* Intense nose, light and soft with long finish.

Viña Los Vascos Ltda

Los Vascos is a small family concern specializing in fine wines for export. Don Jorge Eyzaguirre and his wife Doña María Ignacia Echenique, who own the firm, are both of Basque descent – hence the name.

The Eyzaguirre family first arrived in Chile in 1755, and Don Agustín Eyzaguirre was a member of the Junta which assumed power in Santiago after the deposition of the Spanish Captain-General in 1810 and became its President in 1814, the year of the patriot defeat at Rancagua and the reoccupation of Santiago by the Spaniards. Other distinguished members of the family include Don Jaime Eyzaguirre, the well-known Chilean historian, and Don José María Eyzaguirre, a former President of the Supreme Court. Don Pedro Gregorio Echenique, a Knight of the Order of Santiago, settled in Chile in 1750, and the Echenique family has owned vineyards in the Province of Colchagua since 1772. About 1850 the native País vines were replaced with noble stocks from Bordeaux and Burgundy.

In its present form Los Vascos dates from 1975, when the family bought back vineyards in the Cañetén Valley west of San Fernando which had been segregated during the Allende regime. The valley is particularly suited to viticulture, since it is ringed by mountains, of which the highest is the 3,000-ft high Monte Cañetén, sheltering it from hailstorms in the spring and resulting in summer temperatures ideal for the ripening of the grapes. The average age of the larger part of the vineyards (125 hectares) is forty-five years, and another 45 hectares were planted three years ago. The distribution of grape varieties is:

Cabernet Sauvignon	145 ha
Sémillon	11 ha
Sauvignon Blanc	10 ha
Chardonnay	4 ha

The winery has been modernized under the direction of a distinguished Chilean oenologist now working in California, Don Sergio Traverso, and the day-to-day operation of the winery is conducted by M. Yves Pouzet, a graduate of Montpelier. The Eyzaguirres' son, daughter and son-in-law also play an active part in the running of this most dedicated of family concerns.

The total capacity is 910,000 litres in epoxy-lined concrete vats, 1,290,000 litres in oak and raulí, and 26,500 litres in stainless steel. The wooden containers vary in size from *cubas* of 47,000 litres to 225-litre *barricas*. The white wines are fermented at 15–18°c and the red from 24–28°c.

The old family house built low in Colonial style, with verandas around a patio brilliant with roses, is one of the most beautiful in the area and is a veritable museum housing the relics of the two historic families.

Los Vascos does not sell wine in the domestic market, except in bulk to other wineries, and the emphasis is on fine wines without undue age in wood made for export to the USA, Europe and other countries in South America, where they are sometimes sold as 'Monte Cañetén'.

White Wines

'Chevrier' 1984
60% Sémillon, 40% Sauvignon Blanc. Newly bottled.   *H.J.* Rather neutral nose. Nice balance, plenty acid, good fruit. Slightly harsh, lively. Faint Sémillon finish.   *J.R.* Pale straw. Subdued nose. Big volume of flavour. Ripe, fruity, good balance and finish.   *M.R.* Floral nose. Lively and good long finish.

Sauvignon Blanc 1984 (from tank)
H.J. Nose fresh and typically floral. Not catty. Slight cassis flavour. Good vigorous wine.   *J.R.* Pale straw. Pronounced flowery nose. Lots of delicate fruit. Clean, fresh, lively. Excellent.

Monte Cañetén 1984
80% Sauvignon Blanc, 20% Sémillon. Recently bottled.   *H.J.* Slightly more gold, drier, rounder, flatter (bottle-sick?). 'Sauvignon for elevation, Sémillon for amplitude' – Sergio Traverso. Very good trio of

whites. *J.R.* Less fragrant nose. More of a sharper, apple taste. Harder.

Old Style White
An '82 wine with twelve months in wood. *H.J.* Old, slightly oxidized white. Very dry, not bad. *J.R.* Yellow colour. Slightly oxidized. Oaky and very dry. Maderized finish. *M.R.* Darker colour and maderized in style.

Red Wines

Cabernet Sauvignon 1984
To be aged in French oak. *H.J.* splendid colour. *Clean*, ripe, intense, mid-weight. Concentrated flavours, not at all heavy. Great promise. *J.R.* Dense plum colour. Young, yeasty nose. Masses of fruit. Lots of body and extract. Intense without being heavy. Should develop very well. *M.R.* Bright, damson. Blackberry flavour, full body, long, concentrated, round, intense.
   (tasted two years later, 26.10.86)
J.R. Very deep plum-ruby. Deep blackberry nose. Concentrated fruit. Full body, lots of extract. Good tannin and balance. Long fruit finish. *M.R.* Intense ruby colour. Deep concentrated fruit – blackcurrant jam. Round, very long finish. Wonderful, still a bit tannic. It is more vigorous than the '83, which is a little softer and more velvety, as I remember.

Cabernet Sauvignon 1983
H.J. Much less intense colour. Nose developing. Intense, cassis not grassy but *nerveux*, racy. If only it could be bottled unfiltered. *J.R.* Deep ruby. Fruity nose. Intense blackcurrant flavour. Big, mouthfilling wine. Good finish. *M.R.* Lovely blackcurrant nose. Round, satisfactory, big, long finish. Very, very good.
   (tasted two years later, 31.8.86)
J.R. Mid-plum, ruby. Typical slightly over ripe Cabernet nose. Very ripe C.S. flavour. Long fruity finish. Sophisticated, good. *M.T.R.* Wonderful bright ruby colour. Mellow Cabernet Sauvignon nose. Good fruit and very mature for its age. 'Damp leaves'. *L. S-J.* Deep rich ruby. Very slight brown tinge. Damp wood, big nose. Rich dark chocolate taste. Good mouthful for drinking for next eighteen months.

Cabernet Sauvignon 1982
A wine sold in bulk to Viña Santa Rita in 1981. This sample was kept at the bodega and aged for one-and-a-half years in wood and

then in bottle. *H.J.* Lightish, intense flavours. Very lively and *delicate*. Slightly lacking guts and follow-through. Tasted sweeter when drunk at dinner the previous night. *J.R.* Slightly lighter ruby. Good fruity nose. Not much smell of oak. Nice, but not as intense or fruity as the '83. *M.R.* More mature, softer, elegant and a lovely wine. Long, lingering flavour.

Viña Manquehue Ltda

Viña Manquehue, founded in 1927, is a large supplier of everyday drinking wine, some of it put up in miniature bottles, and is headed by the urbane and charming Don José Rabat. The offices and winery are situated in the middle of Santiago – the name means 'The Place of the Condors' – and when we visited them to taste the wines, the Andes seemed to rise sheer behind, the snow-fringed peaks pink in the setting sun.

The firm owns 171 hectares of vineyards in the Maipo Valley, planted with:

Cabernet Sauvignon	71 ha
Sauvignon Blanc	50 ha
Sémillon	20 ha
Riesling	5 ha

To meet its requirements, it also buys grapes from independent farmers and wine for blending.

The capacity of the bodega is 4,218,235 litres in cement and 7,706,214 litres in wood, most of it in the form of large *cubas* and *fudres* made of old raulí. Domestic sales amount to a healthy 223,500 cases, and exports, which began in 1974–5, to some 47,000 cases.

Apart from the wines listed below, Manquehue also makes an inexpensive carbonated sparkling wine, and a sweet sherry-type wine.

White Wines

Chardonnay 1984
Made from grapes grown in *parronales* (see p.52) in Pirque and cold-fermented. *H.J.* Very white, full-bodied, dry, good clean wine. *J.R.* Fruity nose and flavour. Quite brisk. Nice. *M.R.* Good nose and body, brisk.

Chardonnay 1984 (from the cask)
Grown in *espalderas* at Raco in the Maipo Valley. *H.J.* Slight colour, slight peardrop nose. Ripe, slightly sweet, a little harsh. Perhaps

short. *J.R.* More flowery, more intense flavour. Lots of guts, but somewhat harsh. *M.R.* More fruit in nose. Intense fruity flavour.

Sémillon 1984

From vineyards near Peralillo. Wine not yet finished. *H.J.* Very pale, clean and well-made. Slightly harsh. Good body. *J.R.* Less flowery than the Chardonnay. More acidic. Good quality. *M.R.* Healthy, good body.

Reservado Blanco 1981/82 (39 cc bottle)

Sémillon based, this wine sells a million bottles a month and is available for 13 cents a bottle in the USA. *H.J.* Cheap SO_2 nose. Slight traditional Bordeaux flavour. Neutral but passable. *J.R.* Smells of varnish and sulphur. Rather rough and not very fruity. *M.R.* A bit of sulphur in the nose. Drinkable, but without character.

Red Wines

Cabernet Sauvignon 1984

From Cunaco in the San Fernando Valley. Not yet filtered. *H.J.* Light colour. Nose out of condition – SO_2. Very harsh, slightly bitter, but good fruit. Light. *J.R.* Yeasty nose and flavour. Very young indeed. A lot of fruit, but rough and unfinished. *M.R.* Damson colour. Some fruit in the nose. Lots of extract, but hard to taste the Cabernet Sauvignon. Grip at end. Unfinished.

'El Condo' Cabernet Sauvignon 1984

From near San Fernando. *H.J.* Equally pale. Cleaner and fruitier nose. Nice and lively. Unfinished, but good. *J.R.* Again very yeasty. Lots of fruit, but unfinished. *M.R.* Damson colour. Good fruit and softer. Easy to drink.

'Alcande Jufre' 1980 (home market)

Cabernet Sauvignon. Aged for one year in 9,000-litre *cubas*. *H.J.* Decent lightish red. Unattractive nose. Weak, not clean fruit. Soft, slight vinegar, pleasant texture, easy but feeble. *J.R.* Ruby. Fruity, but penetrating flavour tasting a bit of licorice. Not very nice wood. A bit sweet. *M.R.* Sweetish nose. Thinner, easy to drink, but commercial.

'Premium José Rabat' 1980

Cabernet Sauvignon. *H.J.* Same colour, same vinegar/wood smell. Smooth, richer, mellow. Not unpleasant, but very dull. *J.R.* Dark cherry. Light nose. Not much intensity, but smooth and easy to drink. *M.R.* Smooth, rather sweet and quite good.

Note: The first winery to introduce sweetish red wines was Viña Santa Rita; Manquehue followed, and they are very popular in the north of Chile.

Reservado Rabat 1981/82 (39 cc bottle)

This is a very inexpensive wine priced at 40 cents a bottle in the USA. *H.J.* Clean nose, decent colour. Thin and slightly sweet; more winery than French *vin ordinaire*. Faintly mulled. *J.R.* Dark cherry-red. Animal nose. Sweetish and dilute. *M.R.* Spicy but acceptable everyday drinking.

Espumante Tinto Gasificado

Made from Cabernet Sauvignon, Merlot and 15% Torontel, and aerated with carbon dioxide. *H.J.* Red. No.

Viña Ochagavía SA

Early in the nineteenth century, when Chile was on the verge of declaring independence, Don Silvestre Ochagavía y Sequeiro, Brazilian by birth and of Basque parentage, bought an estate near Santiago and planted it with native vines. No doubt, the birth of the Republic and the victories of Chacabuco and Maipú were toasted with his wines.

His son, Don Silvestre Ochagavía Errázuriz, has been called the Father of the Chilean Wine Industry, since it was he who first introduced French vines and wine-making methods, founding Viña Ochagavía in 1851 (see Chapter 2).

The firm now belongs to Viña Santa Carolina (q.v.). Only 95 hectares of the original vineyards of Santa Rosa del Peral remain. Located in the Maipo Valley 12 km to the south-west of Santiago, they are planted with the black Cabernet Sauvignon and Pinot Noir, and the white Chardonnay, Sauvignon Blanc and Sémillon. The winery at Santa Rosa makes some 3 million litres of wine annually, buying most of the fruit from local farmers. Storage capacity in cement and wood amounts to about 5 million litres.

Average annual sales amount to 400,000 cases in the domestic market and 10,000 cases abroad. In 1980 and 1981 alone, its wines gained six gold medals, four silver medals and two bronze medals at the Bristol Wine Fair.

Tasting notes for some of the Ochagavía wines will be found under Viña Santa Carolina.

The full list of its labels is:

Red wines
'Antigua Reserva Ochagavía'
'Gran Reserva Planella'
'Don Silvestre'
'Envejido'
'Gran Vino Ochagavía'
'Cabernet Planella'

White wines
'Antigua Reserva Ochagavía'
'Gran Reserva Planella'
'Don Silvestre'
'Gran Vino Ochagavía'
'Gran Vino Blanc de Blanc de Planella'

Viña San Pedro SA

Viña San Pedro is one of the 'Big Four' Chilean wine companies (*see p.84*) with a 19 per cent share of the market for nationally sold brands. It also controls two associated firms, Vinos de Chile SA – Vinex (q.v.) and Urmeneta (q.v.).

Its origins go back to 1701, when Don Cayetano Correa acquired an estate at Molina, near Curicó, but the date of foundation is usually given as 1865, since it was then that Don José Gregorio and Don Bonifacio Correa Albano introduced noble vines from France and employed French experts to make the wines. In the van of progress, the family engaged another eminent French oenologist, Professor Pacottet, at the turn of the century, who in 1907 installed at San Pedro the first refrigeration unit in the world for the treatment and betterment of wines. Another first was the largest ever single exportation of Chilean wine – all of 10,700,000 litres to France in September 1958 in the vessel *Charlton Venus*.

Meanwhile, the Correa family had sold the winery in 1941 to the three families of Stein, Wagner and Chadwick (*see p.109*). In mid-1980 it was bought by the Chilean group BHC in partnership with the great Spanish conglomerate, RUMASA. This was not the happiest period, since, as part of its commercial drive, RUMASA experimented in blending Chilean wine with cheap Spanish Valdepeñas. Shortly before its expropriation by the Spanish government, RUMASA sold out, and the company is securely in Chilean hands again.

San Pedro owns three adjoining estates in the Molina – Lontué zone, at San Pedro, San Miguel and La Huerta, amounting in all to 1,079 hectares. Some 330 hectares are planted with Sauvignon Blanc and Cabernet Sauvignon (150 hectares in the traditional *espalderas* and 180 in the Argentine-style *parronales*), and in the near future another 370 hectares are to be planted with Riesling, Chardonnay and Merlot, at present growing in the company's nurseries. Yields of Sauvignon Blanc amount to 25,000 kg/ha from the *parronales* and 17,000 kg/ha from the *espalderas*, and for the Cabernet Sauvignon, 18,000 kg/ha from the *parronales* and 14,000 kg/ha from the *espalderas*. Like the other big concerns, San Pedro buys in large quantities of grapes and wine.

There are large vinification plants at Molina and Los Lirios, further north, with extensive refrigeration facilities. Together with further storage capacity in Santiago, Lontué, Punta Arenas and Antofagasta, the total capacity is 46,660,000 litres, 37,170,000 litres in cement and 9,490,000 litres in oak or raulí.

Annual sales in the domestic market amount to 34 million litres, 70 per cent red wine and 30 per cent white. The wines have for long been exported to most of the countries in South America. Other important export markets are the USA and Japan, and in smaller amounts San Pedro exports its wines to all five continents. Its best-selling export wines are 'Gato Negro' and 'Gato Blanco', very similar in their export versions to 'Llave de Oro'.

Another popular brand in the USA is 'Amigo', in its boldly labelled skittle-shaped bottles. Available as white, rosé and red, it is slightly sweetened and carbonated in the manner of the Portuguese 'Mateus'.

White Wines

'Gata de Oro' Chardonnay 1986 (tasted 31.8.86)
L. S.-J. Good straw colour, pétillant? Fresh full fruity nose, guava. Taste prickly + fruit (*vinho verde*). Very good. Long crisp aftertaste.   H.M. Pale straw, brilliant. Clean dry powerful nose. Elegant, dry rich (Burgundian). Long finish. Fine wine.   J.R. Pale straw. Pronounced flower nose – peachy? Slight pétillance. Strong fruity flavour. Slight sharpness and longish finish.

'Llave de Oro Exportación ' 1984
100% Sauvignon Blanc from Lontué. 12.65° alcohol, total acidity 3.48 g/litre, 46 mg/litre free SO_2, reducing matter 1.98 g/litre.   H.J. Ripe fruit to smell. Round, neutral, *faintly* varietal. Clean finish.   J.R. Fairly concentrated nose. Flowery, pleasant.   M.R. Pale yellow. Good Sauvignon nose. Soft flavour and finish.

'Gato Blanco' Sauvignon Blanc 1984 (tasted Dec. 1986)
H.J. Slight Sauvignon Blanc nose. Ripe, faintly 'peardrops' nose. Fairly

119

sweet, very pleasant and satisfying, smooth but without great character or Sauvignon 'bite'.

'Gato Oro' Chardonnay 1984 (tasted Dec. 1986)
H.J. Distinct but not dramatic Chardonnay characteristics well-seasoned with oak. A very clean and well-made, gently fruity and distinctive wine.

Red Wines

Cabernet Sauvignon 1986 (tasted 20.11.86)
Harvested Feb/March 1986, bottled 27.6.86. *J.R.* Deep, opaque, purple-red. Intense blackberry nose and flavour. Rich, full-bodied, tannic. Long full finish. Marvellous young wine. *M.R.* Beautiful Ribena-blackcurrant colour and taste. Full of fruit, big body, lots of tannin. Long and rewarding finish. Wonderfully soft for such a young wine.

Cabernet Sauvignon Exportación 1984
100% Cabernet Sauvignon from Lontué. 12.75° alcohol, total acidity 3.09 g/litre, 31 mg/litre free SO₂, reducing matter 1·44 g/litre. *H.J.* Full clear red. Rather neutral nose. Light, clean. Slightly sweet, slightly coarse. Honest and pleasant. *J.R.* Dark plum. Very plummy nose and taste. Should mature well. *M.R.* Damson colour. Cabernet Sauvignon nose. Gutsy, long finish. Good.

'Gato Negro' 1983
50% Cabernet Sauvignon and 50% Cot rouge from Lontué. 12.24° alcohol, total acidity 3·09 g/litre, 34 mg/litre free SO₂, reducing matter 6·59 g/litre. *H.J.* Good, clean and pleasant Merlot-type nose. Velouté. Good flavour, slight watery texture and shortish. Pleasing. *J.R.* Pleasant and quite successful blend. *M.R.* Cabernet Sauvignon nose, damp leaves, tobacco. Round, soft and nice.
(tasted 31.8.86)
L. S.-J. Rich ruby colour, no signs of age. Good Cabernet nose, closed. Rich black chocolate, not as much weight or fruit as Californian C.S., but full with good long aftertaste. *H.M.* Deep ruby. Rich C.S. blackcurrant nose. Well balanced, but rather closed. Good fruit, long finish.

'Llave de Oro' 1982
100% Cabernet Sauvigon from Lontué. 12.3° alcohol, total acidity 3.20 g/litre, 31 mg/litre free SO₂, reducing matter 1.88 g/litre. *H.J.* Very deep red. Slight woody nose. Quite intense Cabernet Sauvignon. Ripe, but slightly grassy. Mid-weight. Not *entirely* attractive; weakish

finish.   *J.R.* Pleasant Cabernet Sauvignon nose. Good balance with proper acidity and a little oak. Nice. Fails at end.   *M.R.* Good mellow nose with a little wood. Mature strawberry flavour and finish.

'Gato de Oro' 1981 (tasted Dec. 1986)
H.J. Mid-red. Curiously little scent. Oak rather dominant in fairly lean mature flavour. Not bulging with fruit but pleasant resiny finish.

'Castillo de Molina' Cabernet Sauvignon 1981 (tasted Dec. 1986)
H.J. Mid-red. Attractive nose, sweet and resinous. A fairly big robust wine with good tannic thrust. Very well made, enjoyable and a good interpretation of Chilean style.

Hugh Johnson and Maite Manjón at the cellars of Viña San Pedro

'Castillo de Molina' 1979
100% Cabernet Sauvignon from Lontué. 12.34° alcohol, total acidity
3.21 g/litre, 31 mg/litre free SO$_2$, reducing matter 1.9 g/litre.   *H.J.*
Dark mature colour. Mature, not quite fresh nose. Smooth and plaus-
ible without much depth.   *J.R.* Good nose. Smooth and more finish
than the others. Good fruit. Nice.   *M.R.* Good rusty colour. Fruity,
round, long finish but not quite enough depth. Good.

Viña Santa Carolina

Santa Carolina, which owns Viña Ochagavía (q.v.), is one of the 'Big
Four' Chilean wine companies. It was founded in 1875 by Don Luis
Pereira Cotapos and named in honour of his wife, Doña Carolina
Iñiguez de Pereira. In 1963 it became a public company and now has
some 500 shareholders. The old underground cellars in the Santiago
bodega, with their long aisles and vaulted ceilings, are among the
most atmospheric in Chile and have been named a National
Monument.

The company owns 90 hectares of vineyards at San Alberto de
Malloa near Rapel, 130 km south of Santiago, planted with black
Cabernet Sauvignon, Merlot and Cot, and white Sauvignon Blanc and
Sémillon. Its 85 hectares at Plazuela de los Toros in the Maipo Valley,
15 km from the centre of Santiago, are planted with Cabernet
Sauvignon, Chardonnay, Sauvignon Blanc and Sémillon. Santa
Carolina also draws on fruit from a further 900 hectares of vineyards
belonging to associated firms and to private proprietors from whom
it buys regularly. Of these, 250 hectares in the Maipo region produce
Sémillon, Sauvignon Blanc, Cabernet Sauvignon and 'Bordeaux' (*see
p.49*); 340 hectares near Rapel are planted mainly with Sémillon,
Cabernet Sauvignon and Cot; and 300 hectares in the Maule region
further south supply Cabernet Sauvignon and Sémillon. All the
vineyards not owned by the company are supervised by its
agronomists.

Average yields are:

Cabernet Sauvignon	7,000 litres/ha
Cot	8,000 litres/ha
Pinot Chardonnay	8,000 litres/ha
Sauvignon Blanc	11,000 litres/ha
Sémillon	13,000 litres/ha

Like the other big firms, Santa Carolina also buys large amounts of
wine for blending.

There are three vinification plants with a total throughput of
12,500,000 kg of grapes, situated in Molina near Curicó, in Polonia

in the Rapel region, and in the Plazuela de los Toros on the outskirts of Santiago. The total storage capacity is some 26 million litres: 9 million in cement, 17 million in wood, and 250,000 litres in stainless steel. The wooden containers range in size from *cubas* of 60,000 litres to casks of 850 litres and are made of *encina* (evergreen oak), American oak and raulí. Eight temperature-controlled stainless steel tanks of 20,000 litres capacity are used for the cold fermentation of white wines at harvest time, and for the rest of the year for making sparkling wine by the Charmat method.

Santa Carolina began exporting its wines in 1978, first selling in the Latin American market. It now ranks fourth in size of the exporters, with average annual sales of 70,000 cases, sending its wines to more than twenty countries, including the USA, Belgium, Germany, Australia and Japan. The first of numerous medals gained in international exhibitions was in Paris in 1889.

White Wines

'Gran Vino Blanco' Exportación 1984
100% Sémillon. *H.J.* Fresh and good. Typical Sémillon. *J.R.* Pleasant flowery nose. Delicate fruity flavour. Good balance, well-made. Nice. *M.R.* Good fruit and acidity.

'Don Silvestre' 1984 (Ochagavía)
100% Sauvignon Blanc. Residual sugar 2.5 g/litre. *H.J.* Very nice, fruity, slightly sweet, clean, good. *J.R.* Very pronounced flowery nose. Clean fruit. Excellent. *M.R.* Fruity nose. Ripe fruit. Good body and finish. Very good.

'Estrella de Oro' 1984
100% Chardonnay. *H.J.* Good body, slight acetone, rather neutral but very satisfactory. *J.R.* Refined Chardonnay nose. Good flavour and fruit. *M.R.* Aromatic. Fruity flavour and finish. Good.

'Don Silvestre Blanco' 1982 (Ochagavía)
40% Sémillon, 60% Sauvignon Blanc. *H.J.* Dry, oaky, *clean*, neutral. Well-made old style. *J.R.* Fragrant. Oak + fruit nose and flavour. Quite nice balance. Pleasant. *M.R.* Clean, fruity and fresh. Good.

'Reserva de Familia' 1978
100% Chardonnay, *H.J.* Very oaky, rather good, *ajerezado*, long sweet finish. *J.R.* Clean oak + fruit nose. A good deal of oak, but nicely blended with fruit. Long finish.

Red Wines

Gran Vino Tinto Exportación 1984 (Ochagavía)
100% Cabernet Sauvignon from the Maipo Valley. *H.J.* Mid-red.
Nice fresh, sweet, plummy, not big nose. Mid-body, very sound,
slightly spicy, not very strong. *J.R.* Plummy colour. Nice young
nose. Extremely fruity, sweet and good. *M.R.* Good nose. Medium
body, brisk and good fruity finish.

'Don Silvestre Tinto' 1982 (Ochagavía)
100% Cabernet Sauvignon from the Rapel Valley. *H.J.* Good red.
Strong oak flavours, dried out fruit, thin. *J.R.* Not a very pronounced
nose – oak + fruit. Pretty dry finish. Oak spoils the fruit.

'Antigua Reserva Tinto' 1981 (Ochagavía)
100% Cabernet Sauvignon from the Maipo Valley. *H.J.* Good blend,
very oaky, but ripe fruit flavours. Better finish. Bigger. *J.R.* More
pronounced nose. More fruit and flavour. Fairly acidic. Better than
the '82.

'Estrella de Oro Tinto' 1979
100% Cabernet Sauvignon from the Maipo Valley. *H.J.* Rather light,
very clean oak. Slightly burnt background helps finish. *J.R.* Good
Cabernet Sauvignon nose and flavour. Ripe fruit. Concentrated. A little
light in body, but very nice and the best of the older wines. *M.R.*
Good fruity nose, flavour and finish.

'Reserva de Familia Tinto' 1976
100% Cabernet Sauvignon from the Maipo Valley. *H.J.* Very mature,
rather acid, too developed. *J.R.* Oaky nose. Oaked flavour. Acidity
and astringency. Over its peak. *M.R.* Woody nose, oaky flavour
and very dry finish.

Viña Santa Rita

The family of García Huidobro had owned the estate long before they
founded Viña Santa Rita in 1880. The historic old house, in its park
near Buin, is one of the most beautiful in Chile. Shaded by huge trees,
in a garden where roses, hydrangeas and ferns run riot, it is solidly
built of stone with great glassed-in *miradores* in the Basque style. Connected with it is a chapel – there is a gallery with a private entrance
in which the family attended services in the manner of Philip II at
the Escorial in Spain – where Pope Pius X conducted mass when he
visited Chile as archbishop and cardinal.

Opposite
The old house at Viña Santa
Rita, where General
O'Higgins took refuge with
his 'hundred-and-twenty'

The most famous episode in the history of the house occurred in 1814, when its owner, Doña Paula Jaraquemada hid in it General Bernardo O'Higgins and his one hundred and twenty patriots after their defeat by the Spaniards at the Battle of Rancagua (*see p.28*). It is because of this that Santa Rita's best-known wines are labelled '120'.

Today, the house is only partly occupied, a maze of empty corridors with echoing wooden floors and sparsely furnished rooms. House and garden, with their feeling of *déjà vu*, remind one irresistibly of the damp luxuriance of the Forest of Buçaco in Portugal and its Manueline palace.

In 1978, the García Huidobro family sold the firm to Don Jorge Fontaine, who in turn disposed of it in 1980. It is now a limited company, 50 per cent owned by the American glass manufacturer Owens-Illinois, which is in turn controlled by United Glass, a subsidiary of the British Distillers' Company. The other 50 per cent of shares are Chilean owned, the principal shareholder and President being Don Ricardo Claro Valdés, himself the largest manufacturer of glass bottles in Chile.

The company owns 145 hectares of vineyards in the Maipo valley near Buin and has long-term contracts with the proprietors of another 773 hectares in Colchagua. These 718 hectares are planted with:

Cabernet Sauvignon	528 ha
Sauvignon Blanc	98 ha
Chardonnay	18 ha
Other varieties	74 ha

As Santa Rita is one of the biggest wine firms in Chile, it makes large purchases of grapes and wine from independent farmers and producers. Of its total output, some 600,000 litres are from grapes grown in its own vineyards, five million from purchased grapes and 34,400,000 litres from ready-made wine.

There are two vinification plants, one adjoining the house near Buin and another in Lontué, with capacities of seven million and five million litres. Between them, there is a capacity of 245,000 hl in cement vats, 40,000 hl in wood (of which 2,500 hl is in new French oak casks) and 1,100 hl in stainless steel. Over recent years there has been thoroughgoing modernization of the wineries, as a result of which the Chardonnay, for example, is now vinified one-third in one year-old French oak casks and two-thirds in stainless steel, and then blended.

Santa Rita is perhaps the fastest-growing wine company in the country, and according to the latest figures now leads the national brands with 28 per cent share of the domestic market as against 24 per cent for Concha y Toro. Since the reorganization of its winemaking exports have increased from 17,551 cases in 1984 to 69,523

Opposite top
The orchards of Viña Canepa

Opposite bottom
Vineyards of Viña Taracapá

in 1986. During 1986 the firm has won a clutch of gold medals in international competitions in England, Yugoslavia, Spain and the USA, but undoubtedly the most resounding success was that of its 1984 'Medalla Real 120' Cabernet Sauvignon at the Gault-Millau Olympiad held in Paris in October 1986, where it received a score of 16.6 points out of 20, the highest of all the 36 Cabernets evaluated, including a 1983 Domaine du Chevalier and a 1982 Lynch Bages.

White Wines

Sauvignon Blanc 1985 (tasted 10.10.86)
J.R. Pale straw. Beautiful flowery nose. Fruity, delicate, good acidity and finish. Lovely young dry white wine.

'120 Tres Medallas' 1983
75% Sémillon, 25% Sauvignon Blanc. 12.3° alcohol.   *H.J.* Very pale, Flowery nose. Attractively fruity, very dry. A bit coarse. Poor finish, slight wood.   *J.R.* Flowery nose. Delicately fruity flavour. Trace of oak.

Red Wines

Cabernet Sauvignon 1984 (tasted 22.10.86)
12° alcohol.   *J.R.* Deep ruby. Good Cabernet Sauvignon nose with a little oak. Deep and fruity flavour with plenty of tannin. Long finish. Very nice young wine.

Cabernet Sauvignon 1983 (tasted 31.8.86)
J.R. Deep plummy colour. Good fruity C.S. nose. Deep blackberry flavour. Luscious, full body. Long fruity finish. Very good young wine, should improve in bottle.   *M.R.* Deep ruby colour, robust C.S. nose, some wood, very tannic, spicy finish, robust and very good.   *I.F.* Deep ripe dark red. Nose fragrant and scented, St Emilion/Pomerol. Slightly oaky. Powerful aftertaste, will age well.   *H.M.* Deep ruby plum, rich cigar-box nose. Rich in fruit and tannin. Long finish, fine wine.

'120 Tres Medallas' 1982
One year in American oak.   *H.J.* Good colour. Clean and firm. Good concentration. Has backbone and balance. Good.

'120 Medalla Real' 1979

100% Cabernet Sauvignon. One year in bottle and the rest in large wooden *cubas*. H.J. Pleasant, mature, slightly salty, savoury flavour. Just a bit too old. J.R. Old oak, raisin nose. Fruity, raisins, but drying out a bit. Quite pleasant. M.R. Nice deep nose, fruit and extract, but going downhill. Dry in the mouth.

'Casa Real' 1975

100% Cabernet Sauvignon from selected area. Aged in large oak *cubas* with a further year in *barrica* and one in bottle. H.J. Much better, firmer, younger than the '79. Only *just* over the hill. Very good vintage. J.R. Brick red with brown rim. Nice nose. A lot of mature fruit. Intense, a good old *reserva*. Drying out a bit, but in much better whack than the '79. Perhaps blended with younger wine? M.R. Fruity nose and good body, but the finish is rather dry. You would not think that it was older than the '79. Very good.

Viña Taracapá Ex Zavala

The company was founded in 1874 under the name of Viña Zavala. One of the smaller concerns, it is noted for the quality of its red wines, which are among the best thought-of in Chile.

It owns 70 hectares of vineyards, planted on the very verge of the Andes in the Maipo Valley near Santiago. Grape varieties are:

Cabernet Sauvignon	40 ha
Sauvignon Blanc	20 ha
Pinot Noir	10 ha

All the wine is fermented in 8,000-litre oak *cubas*, about twenty to thirty years old and relatively young by Chilean standards. The total storage capacity, all in wood, is three million litres. Average annual sales amount to 100,000 cases in the home market and 12,000 abroad.

White Wines

Cosecha 1981

Sémillon and Sauvignon Blanc. 12° alcohol. Six months in oak. J.R. Clear yellow. Fresh appley nose. Fresh and appley with a hint of oak. Brisk, clean, good acidity with nice blend of fruit and oak. Excellent value at its very modest price. M.R. Pale colour, Fragrant appley nose. Pronounced fruity taste of apples. Not much middle, but fresh with clean wood.

'Gran Taracapá White' 1980
Sémillon and Sauvignon Blanc. Three years in oak. 12.5° alcohol. *J.R.* Brilliant yellow. Clean oaky nose. Strong oaky taste. Dry and oaky at end. Well-made of its type. *M.R.* Brilliant colour. Dry. Oaky nose, taste and finish.

Red Wines

Cabernet Sauvignon 1981
Two years in oak and one in bottle. *J.R.* Dark damson. Clean nose, fruit + oak. A big and very dry wine with some astringency at the end. *M.R.* Fruity nose. A big, brisk, fruity wine. Tannic finish, but characteristic and good.

'Gran Tarapacá' 1980
Cabernet Sauvignon 70%, Pinot Noir 30%. Three years in oak and one in bottle. 12.8° alcohol. *J.R.* Deep ruby. Oak + fruit nose, trace of cigar-box from Pinot Noir. Good, fresh Cabernet Sauvignon flavour. Rich and full. Very dry finish. Very good. *M.R.* Ruby colour. Pinot in oak + fruit nose. A rich, big wine, with wood and lots of fruit. Long finish.

Cabernet Sauvignon 1962 (half bottle)
100% Cabernet Sauvignon. Three years in wood and nineteen in bottle. *J.R.* Brick-red with orange rim. Maderized raisin nose, but old Cabernet fairly pronounced. Intense Cabernet flavour, but dried out and over the peak. Evidently first-rate in its prime. *M.R.* Fruit + oak nose. Cabernet Sauvignon flavour, but drying out. Becoming a museum piece.

Viña Undurraga SA

One of the Chilean firms best known abroad because it has for long been exporting a large proportion of its wine, Undurraga was founded in 1885 by the aristocratic Don Francisco Undurraga. How he bought vines from France and Germany and obtained Bosnian oak for making casks has already been described in Chapter 2. The firm is still 80 per cent family-owned. It is at present headed by Don Pedro Undurraga, three of whose sons are actively involved: Don Alfonso, as General Manager; Don Fernando, as Administrator; and Don Pedro, as Production Manager.

The property at Santa Ana in the Maipo Valley was bought at public auction in 1882; Doña Isadora Goyenechea de Cousiño, cofounder of Viña Cousiño Macul, also had her eye on it, but arrived late at the sale, and Don Francisco turned down her offer of an additional 100,000 pesos to buy it from him. Water for irrigation was brought from a nearby canal, and with his agronomist, a M. Pressac, Don Francisco supervised the planting of the first vines in person.

The 195 hectares at present under vines are planted with:

Cabernet Sauvignon	70 ha
Sauvignon Blanc	60 ha
Riesling	35 ha
Pinot Noir	20 ha
Chardonnay	10 ha

The long, low-built family house, with its slender colonnades, round, turreted tower and metal roof, is sited in landscaped gardens and is one of the most beautiful Colonial residences in Chile. Once the scene of great aristocratic gatherings – it was here that the founder, Don Francisco, entertained the President of the Republic and his ministers – the house is no longer occupied by the family, but there are plans for its restoration in the near future.

Not far from the house are the bodegas which, again, are among the most atmospheric in the country. The old bodega, built in Colonial style with whitewashed walls, low-pitched tiled roofs and arched doorways, was constructed on the same plan as that of Don Francisco's friend Maximiano Errázuriz at Panquehue and equipped with wine-making plant from France. It houses extensive underground cellars in which the wines are matured, both in wood and bottle, at temperatures which remain between 12°c and 15°c the year round. Adjoining the old bodega and, like it, surrounded by beds of roses and brilliantly flowering shrubs, is a modern plant with the latest in bottling and refrigeration machinery. The total capacity is 6,240,000 litres in epoxy-coated cement; 2,150,000 litres in oak and raulí, ranging from large *cubas* to 225-litre Bosnian oak *barricas*; and 650,000 litres in epoxy-coated steel tanks.

Average annual sales amount to 450,000 cases in the domestic market, but Undurraga has always taken pride in the high proportion of its wine which is exported. At 75,000 cases, exports currently amount to 40 per cent of total production – higher, proportionately, than for any other firm. The wines go to more than fifty countries, especially to South America and the USA. Wines for export (but not for the home market) are bottled in a *caramayola*, a flagon similar in shape to the German *bocksbeutel* – no doubt a legacy of Don Francisco's forays in Germany. Between 1910 and 1981, Undurraga won more than forty gold and silver medals for its wines, and over the last ten years it has gained gold medals in Yalta, Paris, London and Bristol.

White Wines

Riesling 1983

H.J. Very light straw. Nice ripe, slightly peachy nose. Neutral. Fairly full-bodied, not *too* dry – finish a bit awkward. Pleasant.   *J.R.* Typical fruity nose with trace of sulphur. Flavour dry and spoilt by SO_2.   *M.R.* Pretty colour. Not much nose or smell of Riesling. Gentle, neutral and soft. Dry finish.

Sauvignon Blanc 1983

H.J. Very pale. Ripe nose, nice balance and cut. Clean, good balance, but no Sauvignon Blanc character.   *J.R.* Not very pronounced nose. Very dry, a bit acid. Not particularly characterful.   *M.R.* A little mercaptan in the nose. Good fruit and middle. Long finish.

'Viejo Roble' 1977

Don Pedro Undurraga, a portrait of his illustrious ancestor, Don Francisco Undurraga, founder of the firm, with his wife, in background

One to two years in oak.   *H.J.* Darkish yellow. Good, clean, oaky soft and not too dry. Quince flavour.   *J.R.* Perfumed oaky nose. Clean blend of oak + fruit. More characterful than the others. A pleasant wine in traditional style.   *M.R.* Dark colour. Fruit + oak, nicely blended. Good body. Quince flavour. Nice finish. Very good.

Rosé Wine

Rosé
Pink Cabernet. 12° alcohol, residual sugar 9 g/litre.   *H.J.* Very pale.
Pretty nose. Much too sweet.   *J.R.* Pale orange. Pleasant enough
nose. A bit sweet and flabby.   *M.R.* Pretty colour, but too sweet.

Red Wines

Cabernet Sauvignon 1982
No oak – kept in epoxy-coated steel and then for one year in bottle.
Sells for $2.99 in the USA.   *H.J.* Mid-red. Good fresh typical varietal.
Slightly grassy nose. Plenty of body, not heavy – attractive if not
very vigorous.   *J.R.* Deep ruby. Authentic fruity Cabernet Sauvignon
nose. Soft, fruity blackberry taste. Very nice.   *M.R.* Good Cabernet
nose, not too intense. Soft, very ripe fruit. Short finish?

Pinot Noir 1979
75% Pinot Noir, 25% Cabernet Sauvignon. Fermented in cement and
kept in old (50 year-old) oak, with a further two years in bottle. Sells
in the USA for $5.00.   *H.J.* Darker than the '82. Attractively woody
nose. Delicious hint of old-style Burgundy in flavour. Good mid-
weight and length. Very successful. Tobacco leaf aromas, not *too* dry.
Could be more fleshy.   *J.R.* Ruby with orange rim. Very pleasant
cigar-box nose. Lots of body, fruity, good finish. Very good. *M.R.*
Pretty orange colour. Soft Pinot nose. Deep, Burgundy-type flavour.
Elegant. Long. Very good.

Special Selection 'Viejo Roble' 1977
100% Cabernet Sauvignon.   *H.J.* Slight mercaptan/wood nose. Big,
but flavour dried and narrowed to astringency from rich, very ripe
Cabernet Sauvignon. Rather short/weak finish.   *J.R.* Brick-red with
orange rim. Oak + fruit nose with slight mercaptan, Still healthy, but
drying out somewhat and a bit lacking in fruity flavour. Finish mainly
oak.   *M.R.* Good nose, wood a bit pronounced. Big wine, good
balance, finish a bit oaky. Past its best.

Viñedos Ortiz SA – Viña Linderos

Viña Linderos was founded in 1865 by Don Alejandro Reyes Cotapos,
a well-known lawyer and politician, who was at various times President of the Senate, President of the Supreme Court, Minister of Commerce, Interior Minister and Minister for Foreign Affairs. He was also

a pioneer in introducing vines and vinification methods from Europe.

Control of the firm later passed to the Ortiz family, of whom the first representative was Don Miguel Ortiz Olave. Born in another famous wine region, the Rioja in Spain, he emigrated to Chile in 1910 and by 1918 was planting noble grape varieties at Linderos, near Buin in the Maipo Valley. His son, Don Eugenio Ortiz Iriondo, was Professor of Oenology at the Universidad Católica in Santiago between 1940 and 1952 and undertook a thorough modernization of the winery during the 1960s. The concern is now run by his three sons, all with impressive qualifications in oenology: Don Miguel Ortiz Lizarralde, Don Eugenio Ortiz Lizarralde and Don Juan Manuel Ortiz Lizarralde.

Like other of the wine firms, Linderos is also a large producer of fruit, especially dessert grapes, plums and nectarines, which it exports to the USA.

The vineyards, sited in the very shadow of the Andes, are irrigated with water from the Maipo river and extend to 81 hectares, planted with:

Cabernet Sauvignon	45 ha
Sauvignon Blanc	14 ha
Sémillon	11 ha
Chardonnay	7 ha
Riesling	4 ha

The red wines are fermented in cement, and the white in large wooden *cubas*. In both cases there are means of controlling the temperature, The firm bottles and labels its wine only to order, the minimum being for fifty bottles. It has been shipping them abroad since 1884, and average annual sales run to 33,317 cases in the domestic market and 13,212 cases abroad.

White Wines

Chardonnay 1984
100% Chardonnay. Residual sugar 18 g/litre.   J.R. Very pale straw. Fragrant appley nose. Good flavour and fruit. Refreshing. A bit sweet in the middle and at the finish.   M.R. Pale, pale colour. Fragrant appley nose carrying through into the flavour. Finish a bit sweet.

'Otoñal Verde' 1983
50% Sémillon and 50% Sauvignon Blanc.   J.R. Yellow colour. Faint nose. Dry and tart. Little finish.   M.R. Not much fruit in the nose. Very dry. Lacks fruit and finish.

Champaña Rhin 1984
A sparkling wine made from Riesling by the Champagne method.   J.R. Good fruity nose and flavour, but too sweet for a sparkling wine and needs more acid to give it kick.   M.R. Good Riesling nose. Fruity flavour in the middle, but too much sugar and needs more acidity.

Red Wines

Cabernet Sauvignon 1984
J.R. Deep plum. Nice young plummy nose. Good fruit and depth, but finish a bit astringent.   M.R. Blackberry colour, brisk and round. Grip and fruit. Good.

Petit Sirah 1984
Bottled without malolactic fermentation.   J.R. Fruity and rather sweeter. Pleasant.   M.R. Deep and intense bouquet. Quite pleasant.

Cabernet Sauvignon 1983
J.R. Very dark plum. Less fruit in the nose and very dry.   M.R. Darker colour, reasonable fruit and finish, but much on the dry side. (Tasted 16.8.86, the wine was still a deep ruby plum colour but was left with little fruit on the nose, a hard flavour and sharp finish.)

Cabernet Sauvignon 1982
The wine had spent some time in 40,000-litre raulí *cubas*.   J.R. Very dry, a bit acid and without much fruit.   M.R. Some wood in the nose and taste. Fruit reduced by the wood, thin.

Vinos de Chile SA – 'Vinex'

Vinex is now a subsidiary of Viña San Pedro (q.v.), which acquired the winery in 1976. It was founded in 1942 by the Junta de Exportación Agrícola as an export cooperative and from 1942 to 1948 exported most of the branded Chilean wines, as well as its own 'Santa Helena' and 'Vinex'.

'Santa Helena' is still a well-known name, with a market share of some 4 per cent in the national brands category.
Its labels are:

White
Santa Helena 'Siglo de Oro'
Santa Helena Chablis
Santa Helena 'Rhin'

Rosé
Santa Helena Rosé

Red
Santa Helena Cabernet Sauvignon

Vitivinícola Comercial Millahue Ltda

This small firm, founded in 1970, belongs to Professor Hernández of the Universidad Católica in Santiago. It owns 35 hectares of vineyards in the Maipo Valley, planted with 15 ha of Cabernet Sauvignon, 12 ha of Sémillon and 8 ha of Sauvignon Blanc.

The winery at Buin, south of Santiago, has a capacity of 790,000 litres in wood and 210,000 litres in cement. Sales average an annual 7,000 cases in the domestic market and 8,549 cases abroad.

Its labels are:

White wines
'Portal del Alto' Gran Reserva
Sémillon/Sauvignon Blanc
Sémillon Gran Vino
Gran Vino Sémillon/Sauvignon
'Santa Paulina' Gran Vino Blanco
Sémillon

Rosé wines
'Santa Paulina' Gran Vino Rosé
'Rosé del Portal' Gran Vino

Red wines
'Portal del Alto' Gran Reserva
Cabernet Sauvignon
Cabernet Gran Vino
'Santa Paulina' Gran Vino Tinto
Cabernet

THE COOPERATIVES

There are six cooperative wineries in Chile making table wines, all in the more southerly part of the wine-growing area in the VII and VIII Regions, with annual outputs ranging from 12.5 million to 2 million litres.

They are organized in similar fashion, with the *socios* or members supplying grapes from their vineyards to a central winery which vinifies and markets the wine, making payment in the form of a share in the proceeds from sales. Wine may alternatively be returned to the *socio* for private sale. Only two of the cooperatives, those of Curicó and Talca, export any of their wine. The larger proportion is sold to the large private firms for blending, but a certain amount is bottled and sold under the cooperative's own label.

The cooperatives are equipped with cement or wooden receptacles for vinifying and storing the wine, and four of them possess refrigeration facilities. The cement vats are in process of modernization by cladding with epoxy resin, but the wood, mostly raulí, is in general very old and in need of replacement. This is clearly an area in which substantial investment is desirable, so that the cooperatives may make the best use of the excellent fruit.

The production and equipment of the cooperatives is summarized in the table below:

	Capacity (hl)	Production (hl)	White	Red
				TYPES OF WINE
Curicó	180,000	121,110	Sémillon-Sauvignon (50%)	'Bordeaux' (40%) País (10%)
Talca	200,000	125,510	Sémillon-Sauvignon (50%)	'Bordeaux' (35%) País (15%)
Loncomilla	120,000	71,500	Sémillon (20%)	'Bordeaux' (10%) País (70%)
Cauquenes	190,000	102,750	Sémillon (30%)	'Bordeaux' (10%) País (50%) Carignan (10%)
Nuble	60,000	21,430	Sémillon (20%)	País (80%)
Quillón	120,000	80,000	Moscatel (30%) Sémillon (20%)	Cinzaut (10%) País (30%) Cabernet (10%)

'Bordeaux' refers to a blend of Cot, Merlot and Verdot.

Cooperativa Agrícola Vitivinícola de Cauquenes Ltda

The cooperative, one of the largest in Chile with 263 members, is situated in Cauquenes, west of Chillán and only 25 km from the Pacific in the foothills of the Cordillera de la Costa. The area is densely planted with vines, mainly from the native red País, which grow unirrigated in the clays and granitic sands of the hill slopes.

Like the other cooperatives, Cauquenes ferments the wines in cement, using epoxy-coated vats for the better, and matures them in large *cubas* and casks made mainly of raulí.

The bulk of the wine made at the cooperative is inexpensive red País, sold in 5-litre carafes or litre bottles for local consumption. It also sells more mature wines in 700 ml bottles under the label of 'Lomas de Cauquenes' ('*loma*' means 'slope'). The white contains 60 per cent of Sémillon and 40 per cent of Sauvignon Blanc and is aged for six to seven months in raulí; the red is made with 70 per cent País, 15 per cent Carignan and 15 per cent Cabernet and is aged for a year in wood. They are 'country' wines made to the Chilean taste and seem over-oaky and sharp to the foreign palate.

The País wines from this unirrigated area, where yields are low, are, in fact, the best of their type. Without undue age in old wood and time in bottle, they are fruity and full-bodied and make pleasant drinking.

In small amount, the cooperative makes varietal wines from Cabernet Sauvignon, Sauvignon Blanc and Riesling. The quality of such wines may be judged from the notes of a tasting at the adjoining experimental station (*see p.147*) and indicate the very real possibilities for developing viticulture in the region, given adequate investment and a programme for replanting and irrigating the vineyards, and modernizing the wineries.

Cooperative Agrícola Vitivinícola de Curicó Ltda

The cooperative of Curicó in the VII Region, founded in 1939, is well-known for the quality of its wines. Its *socios* or members farm a total of 1,414 hectares of vineyards, planted with:

Sauvignon Blanc	623 ha
Sémillon	426 ha
Cot (or Malbec)	153 ha
Cabernet Sauvignon	145 ha
Riesling	30 ha
Merlot	16 ha
Pinot Noir	12 ha
Chardonnay	9 ha

Average annual sales amount to 346,322 cases and exports to 6,397 cases. It has recently been shipping sizeable quantities of red wine in bulk to Japan.

It was unfortunately not possible to arrange for a systematic tasting of the wines, but if a red reserve drunk at lunch is typical, the cooperative's reputation is certainly justified.

'Los Robles' Gran Reserva Tinto
100% Cabernet Sauvignon. Three years in wood and one in bottle. *J.R.* Bright ruby with orange rim. Good Cabernet Sauvignon nose + a little oak. Clean, light, good Cabernet Sauvignon flavour. Not excessively oaky or too dry. Raspberry finish. Excellent value at 200 pesos (less than £2) in a restaurant. *M.R.* Light, bright ruby. Oaky nose, fruit behind it. Round and good finish.

The other labels are:

White wines
'Gran Roble'
Chardonnay
Sauvignon Blanc
Sémillon

Red wines
'Gran Roble'
Cabernet Sauvignon
Merlot

Cooperativa Agrícola Vitivinícola de Quillón Ltda

This large cooperative is further south off the main road from Chillán to Concepción in the foothills of the Cordillera de la Costa and in the centre of some 40,000 hectares of vineyards, the first of which were planted by the Spaniards in 1580. The vines grow in soils containing some 90 per cent clay with a little sand and are unirrigated. The 1,617 hectares farmed by the members of the cooperative are planted with:

País	679 ha
Moscatel	566 ha
Sémillon	254 ha
Cinzaut	59 ha
Cabernet	59 ha

About 90 per cent of the wine is vinified in cement vats, which, in the case of the better wines, are lined with epoxy resin. The rest of the wine is fermented in wood, and the reds are matured in raulí.

The cooperative also makes brandy in Charentais-type stills.
The labels are:

White wines
'Don Francisco Cauquillón'
'Moscatel de Alejandría'
'Moscatel Dorado'

Red wines
'Gran Vino Don Francisco'
'Don Francisco'

The wines for which the cooperative is best known are its Moscatels, all made with 100 per cent Moscatel de Alejandría. Of the two table wines, the 'Don Francisco Cauquillón', aged for two to three years in oak, is the more fragrant, with a clean and fruity Muscat nose. Perhaps because the wine is fermented at 25°c, nose and flavour tend to disappear in the glass. The younger 'Moscatel de Alejandría', fermented at 18°c with little or no time in wood, is, surprisingly for a Moscatel, a very dry wine containing less than 1 g/litre of residual sugar. The dessert 'Moscatel Dorado' is fortified with grape spirit to 14.5° and very sweet, but is fermented at 26–28°c, and this probably accounts for the subdued nose and flavour.

Of the reds, the most attractive is the young and extremely inexpensive 'Gran Vino Don Francisco', made from 100 per cent País. A pretty damson colour, it has a clean nose with a hint of blackberries and is brisk and fruity. A 1981 'Don Francisco', made from 30 per cent Cabernet Sauvignon and 70 per cent Cinzaut, had lost fruit during a three-year ageing in raulí and was not entirely clean.

Cooperativa Agricola Vitivinícola de Talca Ltda

The cooperative, founded in 1944, is in the town of Talca at the centre of the VII Region, which makes some 53 per cent of all Chilean wine. It numbers 146 *socios*, who, between them, own 1,160 hectares of vineyards planted with:

Sémillon	402 ha
Cabernet Sauvignon	260 ha
Sauvignon Blanc	207 ha
Cabernet Franc	100 ha
Merlot	87 ha
Cot (or Malbec)	33 ha
Pinot Noir	28 ha

The grapes are carefully checked for type and quality on delivery to the cooperative. Different varieties may not be mixed, and substandard fruit is refused. Wine may either be returned to the *socio* for him to sell it privately or may be sold on his behalf by the cooperative, in which case he receives reimbursement.

The capacity of the winery is 14 million litres in cement and 6 million litres in wood. Most of this is in the form of large *cubas* and *fudres* made of raulí, but there are also smaller casks of American oak for maturing the better wines. Its oenologist, Alejandro Parot, is much respected in Chile, and the cooperative is making strenuous efforts to improve its equipment and methods; two of its staff have recently been in France and Spain to study wine-making procedures.

The best of its white wines are fermented at 15–19°c in epoxy-lined cement vats, and the others for local consumption at 27–28°c. The red wines are fermented at 27–28°c in cement *autovinificadores*, working on the principle of a coffee percolator and providing for automatic submersion of the 'cap'.

Some two-thirds of the wine is sold to the large private firms for blending, but the cooperative has recently sold some 60,000 litres of bottled wine in the USA under the label of 'Vinos Exposición'.

The range of wines is very large:

White wines
'Escudo de Talca' (50% Sémillon, 50% Sauvignon Blanc)
'Reserva de Talca' (50% Sémillon, 50% Sauvignon Blanc)
'Conde de Maule' (100% Sauvignon Blanc)
'Chablis Mister Chichi' – export (50% Sémillon, 50% Sauvignon Blanc)
'Sauvignon' – export to Japan (100% Sauvignon Blanc)

The Cooperative at Talca

Rosé wine
'Rosé de Talca' (100% Cabernet Sauvignon)

Red wines
'Escudo de Talca' (100% Cabernet Sauvignon)
'Reserva de Talca' (100% Cabernet Sauvignon)
'Escudo de Talca' – export (100% Cabernet Sauvignon)
'Conde de Maule' (100% Cabernet Franc)
'Mister Chichi' (100% Cabernet Franc)

All of the white wines were clean and extremely dry, and it was perhaps because of the absence of residual sugar and of ageing most of them in raulí that they tended to lack more pronounced nose and fruit. Our favourite (J.R., M.T.R.) was the slightly sweeter 'Reserva de Talca' 1982 without age in wood, with its pleasantly fragrant nose and good fruit and balance.

The red wines were again dry to a degree, and one felt that they would have been cleaner and fruitier without ageing in old raulí for periods of up to two years. Our preference was for export 'Escudo de Talca' 1980. A more recent tasting note (16.11.86) on a younger vintage runs:

'Escudo de Talca' Cabernet Sauvignon NV
J.R. Plum-ruby. Healthy young Cabernet Sauvignon nose. Quite fruity and well-balanced. Brisk, a bit sharp, obviously young, but sound and appetizing. Nice mouthful, quite light, good refreshing uncomplicated young C.S. Shortish finish.

The cooperative also makes large amounts of *chicha* (*see p.55*), sweetish and with a slight bubble, from the País grape.

INIA Subestación Experimental Cauquenes

INIA, the government-run Instituto de Investigaciones Agropecuarias, maintains a network of agricultural stations covering the whole country. The Subestación Experimental de Cauquenes, situated just outside the town of Cauquenes, is particularly concerned with viticulture and the growing of fruit in the VII Region.

It has some 50 hectares under vines and fruit trees, and in the field of wines its investigations centre on drip irrigation (*see p.48*) and the suitability of noble wine varieties from California for plantation in the area.

It possesses an experimental winery (though this is yet to be equipped with temperature-controlled stainless steel fermentation tanks) and well-equipped laboratories, and has recently published the results of a comprehensive survey, *Posibilidades de desarrollo de la vitivinicultura*

Opposite
A stall in the fruit and vegetable market, Santiago

142

de area de Cauquenes, VII Region del Maule, carried out by Dr Lloyd A. Lider of Davis University and Sr Arturo Lavin, the station's oenologist. Their conclusions are that, if the vineyards are irrigated and replanted and the wineries modernized, the region is capable of producing wines as good as, if not better than, any in Chile. (*See also* p.42)

Some of the wines made at the station are on sale in limited quantity.

White Wines

Riesling 1984
100% Riesling fermented at 29–30°c in cement without epoxy lining. 12.6° alcohol, total acidity 4.5 g/litre, 38.4 mg/litre free SO$_2$. J.R. Pale straw. Some fruit in the nose and taste. A touch of sulphur and

Opposite top
Fishing in the cool waters of the Humbolt current off the coast of Chile

Opposite bottom
Dried fruit in the fruit and vegetable market, Santiago

The old *finca* of Don Emilio Merino, of the Federation of Cooperative Wineries, near Cauquenes

145

Drip irrigation of vines on an experimental plot at INIA near Cauquenes

a trace of sugar. Quite nice and very creditable considering the unsophisticated equipment.   *M.R.* Pretty lemon colour. Good fruit, round, a bit sweet at the finish?

Chardonnay 1984 (experimental only)
100% Chardonnay from young plants, again fermented at 27°c.   *J.R.* Pale straw. Quite fragrant nose. Reasonable fruit, but hollow in the middle. Good finish.   *M.R.* Delicate and fresh. Fruit not too marked, but delicate. Good finish.

Red Wines

Cabernet Sauvignon 1984
100% Cabernet Sauvignon. Fermented at 30°c, filtered but not bottled and resting in raulí. 13.4° alcohol, volatile acidity 0·39 g/litre, total

acidity 4.2 g/litre, residual sugar 1.6 g/litre. *J.R.* Deep plum. Not as much fruit as some. Very dry. Some astringency at end. *M.R.* Plum colour, brisk but good.

Cabernet Sauvignon 1982/83/84

A blend of three vintages, fermented without temperature control. The 1982 was kept in wood before coupage. 13.2° alcohol, volatile acidity 0·68 g/litre, total acidity 3.6 g/litre, residual sugar 3.3 g/litre. *J.R.* Plum colour. Smells of wood – almost vinegary. Dry, astringent and without fruit. *M.R.* Not much fruit, woody and vinegary.

'Terciopelo' 1981

70% País, 30% Cot. In wood since the harvest and bottled at the end of October 1984. 12.9° alcohol, volatile acidity 0·72 g/litre, total acidity 4.2 g/litre, 17.7 mg/litre free SO_2, residual sugar 2.2 g/litre. *J.R.* Ruby. País + raulí nose. Not as hard as the others (the name means 'velvet') and more rounded and attractive.

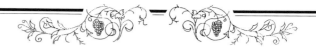

CHAPTER EIGHT

Chilean Cooking

Maite Manjón

Chilean cooking, as it exists today, results from the fusion of three different traditions: the indigenous Indian; creole, or that of the native-born inhabitants of Spanish descent; and foreign, mainly French. You will not find many typical Chilean dishes in fashionable restaurants and hotels or even in private houses, though in all of them the excellent fish and shellfish from the cold waters of the off-shore current are regularly served. They are now to be found mainly in small restaurants in the country districts, in specialized establishments in the cities, or in the homes of the agricultural workers. Only one, the popular *empanada*, is served by rich and poor alike on Sundays.

The cooking of the indigenous Indians was based on the three products which formed the basis of their agriculture; maize (*choclo*), kidney beans (*frejoles*) and potatoes (*papas*) – said to have originated in Chile. In addition, they naturally made use of fish from the Pacific and from the cold waters of the rivers and lakes in the south. Until recently, meat has never, as in the Argentine, been very plentiful. Most traditional of the Indian dishes was *charquicán*, made for religious festivals with vegetables and dried meat (*charqui*), and blessed by the future Pope Pius IX when he was regaled with it on an official visit to Chile in 1824 after the country had gained independence. It remains the only authentic Chilean dish to be included in *Larousse Gastronomique*.

The strongest influence on Chilean cooking has been the Spanish, dating from the time when the Conquistadores and their descendants began introducing cattle, vegetables, fruit trees and vine stocks from Spain. From this period dates the *empanada* or savoury tart; the *cazuelas* or rich stews, so reminiscent of the *ollas* beloved of Don Quixote; and the *pasteleras de maiz*, the pies made with maize flour. It was a hearty and highly seasoned cookery, making much use of spices and onions, garlic and peppers.

Vice-Admiral John Byron has left an amusing account of this fare and of eighteenth-century table manners in his *Narrative* (*see p.27*).

> They eat every thing so highly seasoned with red peppers, that those who are not used to it, upon the first mouthful would imagine their throats on fire for an hour afterwards: and it is a common custom here, though you have the greatest plenty at your own table, to have two or three Mulatto girls come in at the time you dine, bringing, in a little silver plate, some of these high-seasoned ragouts, with a compliment from Donna such-a-one, who desires you will eat a little bit of what she has sent you; which must be done before her Mulatto's face, or it would be deemed a great affront.

As in Spain, the nuns made a variety of sweetmeats in their convents, often from eggs and almonds, and themselves based on recipes derived from the Moors. The tradition has never been lost and was continued by famous cooks such as Doña Matilde Rengifo Rengifo, whose recipies have been preserved in *Recetas de las Rengifo*, now in its sixteenth edition.

French influence on the cuisine began at the time of 'la belle époque' towards the end of the nineteenth century, when François Gage started the first French restaurant in Santiago in the calle Huérfanos. It received impetus from the regular visits of wealthy Chilean families to Paris. They brought back with them furniture, pictures and fabrics, and began building great residences like the Palacio Cousiño in neo-classical style to set them off. Not only were French vine stocks all the rage, but also its cuisine.

Although the French was not the only nineteenth-century foreign influence on the cuisine – the German farmers in the south, for example, introduced their *strudel de manzanas* (*apfelstrudel*) – it has remained the predominant one. In more recent times, with increasing availability of prime meat, steaks sold by weight, American-style, figure on the menus of all the leading hotels and restaurants and are extremely tender and full of flavour. Nevertheless, fish, especially shellfish, including varieties not known in Europe, continues to be the *pièce de resistance* of any Chilean menu, and the fresh fruit is legion. Some of the more exotic varieties are described in the glossary which follows.

It is, however, worth repeating the earlier warning. Fruit and vegetables grown in contact with the soil can cause dire stomach upheavals among those unaccustomed to the Chilean environment. This applies specially to the tempting bowls of strawberries and to green salads. It is always safer to eat fruit with a rind or skin and to peel it yourself. Again, you should ask for bottled water, especially in country districts, and make sure that the cap is removed in your presence.

Foodstuffs and typical dishes

Note: Only dishes and products which are typically of the country have been listed. There are also large numbers of dishes of Spanish origin, e.g. *tortilla* (Spanish omelette), *paella, bacalao a la vizcaina* (dried cod Basque-stye), *riñones al Jerez* (kidneys in sherry), etc.

Aguitas Medicinales	When afflicted by 'Montezuma's Revenge', the answer, apart from prompt recourse to 'Lomatil', is to ring for the chambermaid and to request an 'aguita'. She will bring you an infusion of camomile flowers, mint and herbs, which in most cases of stomach upsets is both soothing and effective. Papaya fruit, too, calms the digestion, though few except masochists will go as far as crunching the strongly alkaline pips, a remedy recommended in extreme cases. Apart from camomile tea for the digestion, there is a range of 'aguitas', including an infusion of lime flowers for colds.
Ají	Everywhere else in the world chillis are known as such, but not in Chile itself!
Albacora	Swordfish.
Almeja	Clam.
Arvejitas	Green peas.
Asado criollo	Barbecued meat, usually lamb.
Café	Coffee. Chile is not a producer of coffee, and it is the custom, even at the best restaurants and hotels, to bring to the table a jug of hot water and a packet of Nescafé. If you want real coffee, you must go to an expresso bar and insist on *café-café, expresso*.
Caldillo de congrio	A soup-like stew made by stewing *congrio* (q.v.) steaks in an earthenware *cazuela* with potatoes, tomatoes, onions, herbs and spices.

Camarones	Prawns.
Camarones del rio	Crayfish. These are large and succulent.
Caracoles	Sea-snails, boiled and eaten cold as an apéritif.
Cazuela de ave	A chicken broth containing small pieces of meat or chicken, together with rice, onion, potatoes and other vegetables.
Cebiche de locos	Also popular in Peru, this is a marinade of minced uncooked abalone in lemon juice and chopped onion, spiced with salt and pepper.
Cecinas	Charcuterie. This comes in the forms familiar in Spain: *jamón ahumado*, resembling Parma ham; *chorizo*, a highly cured pepper sausage, eaten as an apéritif; *longaniza*, a rather similar, but less refined sausage used in cooking.
Centolla	King crab.
Chanco en piedra	A savoury sauce typical of Central Chile made from puréed tomatoes, chopped onions, garlic and spices.
Charquicán	A traditional Indian vegetable stew, of which the main ingredients are potatoes, squash and sweetcorn. It is now usual to add onion, carrot, peas and a little minced meat.
Chirimoya	A fruit looking somewhat like a large avocado pear. Here the resemblance ends, since it is peeled, the large pips are removed, and it is then cut like a pineapple into thick, juicy slices. The flavour is rather similar, though more delicate.
Choclo	Maize, sweetcorn.
Chupe de locos	Similar to *Chupe de mariscos* (q.v.), but containing only *locos* (abalone).
Chupe de mariscos	A rich stew of mixed shellfish cooked in sauce containing breadcrumbs and grated cheese.
Color	A favourite orange-coloured sauce made by heating garlic and paprika in melted fat or cooking oil, and either hot or mild to taste.
Congrio	This does not mean conger eel, as in a Spanish dictionary, but is the name of a

151

long, cylindrical fish considered a great delicacy in Chile. The steaks may be served boiled or fried, or in the form of *caldillo de congrio* (q.v.).

Corvina al horno rellena There is no translation for *corvina* (*Cilus montii*) a fish very popular in Chile. In this version, it is stuffed with minced *longaniza*, a cured sausage, together with onion, vegetables and spices, and baked.

Curanto Similar to *pulmai* (q.v.), but cooked in an open pot placed over hot stones in a hole in the ground and covered with large leaves.

Durazno A peach.

Empanadas Equally popular in Argentina, these are small pasties, usually eaten before a meal and especially on Sundays. A variety of fillings may be used, but they frequently contain chopped meat, fried onions, raisins and olives. They may either be baked in the oven or fried.

Erizo A large sea urchin, bigger than any found in Europe, some four inches or more across. The edible parts are five strips of yellow-orange flesh. Delicious in the form of a mousse, *erizo* may be bought canned.

Fruit Apart from the exotic varieties listed separately, most of the fruit familiar in Europe is grown in Chile, including: apples, pears, plums, peaches, nectarines, cherries, apricots, medlars, quinces, oranges, lemons, melons, raspberries, strawberries, blackberries, figs and gooseberries.

Humitas A traditional Indian dish made by grating sweetcorn, mixing it with butter and chopped onion, spicing it with basil and other herbs, then wrapping small portions of the savoury mixture in the corn husks and boiling them.

Jaiba An ugly-looking, but entirely delicious crab-like shellfish (*Cancer edwardsii*), boiled and eaten cold with mayonnaise.

Kiwi Originally a native of China, this refresh-

	ing fruit was introduced to Chile in 1974, where it has since flourished.
Loco	Abalone. A shellfish found the length of the Pacific coast. It may be boiled and eaten cold; alternatively, it is minced or chopped and used in other dishes. It is also canned.
Lucuma	A green, round fruit of medium size, native to South America, with yellow, sweet-smelling flesh.
Macha	A clam-like shellfish (*Mesodesma donacium*).
Miel de palma	This 'honey', popular in Chile, is not made by bees, but from palm sap, coconut milk and sugar. It is sold in small tins.
Milcao	A bread made with potato flour and used with *curanto* (q.v.).
Nispero	A loquat.
Paila chonchi	A dish reminiscent of *bouillabaisse*, but with more substance and more ingredients.
Palta	An avocado pear, sp. *aguacate*.
Papa	A potato.
Papas al aji	Mashed potato with chilli.
Papaya	Smaller and more fragrant than the tropical papaya or pawpaw of Brazil, Peru and Ecuador, the Chilean variety cannot be eaten fresh, but is boiled and bottled in syrup. In this form it is luscious and very sweet. The juice is also canned and drunk as a soft drink or used as a mixer with pisco (*see Chapter 6*).
Pastel de choclo	One of the best of Chilean corn dishes, made like a shepherd's pie with minced meat, but topped with ground fresh sweetcorn. It is baked until the crust is crisp on the top, and the sweetish flavour of the corn contrasts well with that of the meat.
Pebre	A popular Chilean sauce made of onions, vinegar, olives, garlic, chilli and coriander. Used like ketchup, it is much better and goes well with most meat dishes.
Poroto	A small dried white bean, native to Chile.

Porotos granados	Of Indian origin, this delicious vegetable stew contains *porotos*, sweetcorn and squash, enlivened with onion, garlic and spices.
Postres	Desserts. Most of the desserts are of foreign origin, many of them Spanish. Perhaps the best are the tarts and iced cakes made with fresh fruit; and fruit itself, in its huge variety, makes a pleasant finish to a meal. Try the *chirimoya* (q.v.) or bottled *papaya* (q.v.).
Pulmai	A mixture of shellfish steamed in the shell with onions, spices and meat or chicken.
Queso	Cheese. Most of the cheese is of familiar foreign type: Gruyère, Roquefort, Camembert, etc., but the IV Region north of Santiago produces a good local goat cheese.
Zumo de naranja	Fresh orange juice is plentiful and first-rate. When ordering it at breakfast, ask for *zumo de naranja natural* to ensure that it *is* fresh, and not bottled or canned.

Some typical recipes

Cebiche de Locos (Marinade of Abalone)

SERVES SIX

If you live in a country like Australia or the USA, use fresh abalone; otherwise sea scallops may be substituted. *Cebiche* may also be made with any firm white fish, such as turbot, halibut, etc.

1 kg fresh locos (abalone) or sea scallops, cleaned and cut into 1 inch pieces
Salt and pepper, freshly ground
1 onion, chopped very fine

250 ml fresh lemon juice ⎫ *mixed*
250 ml fresh lime juice ⎭
Dash of ají de color *(see below)*
1 large tablespoon chopped parsley
1 clove chopped garlic

Place the fish in a flat glass dish and pour over it a marinade made from the rest of the ingredients. If not completely covered, add more lemon juice. Cover the dish and leave it in the refrigerator until the next day. Serve on a bed of lettuce.

To make ají de color

This spicy red sauce may be kept for up to a month in a bottle in the refrigerator. The following quantities will make 1 pint.

250 ml dry red chillis pressed down	1 clove squeezed garlic
6 dl boiling water	140 ml olive oil
½ teaspoon salt	250 ml boiling water

Chop the dry chillis into small pieces and soak for ½ hour. Always wash your hands thoroughly with soap and hot water after handling them.

Remove the seeds of the chillis, place them in a bowl with the first 6 dl of boiling water, leave for 3 hours and drain. Add all the other ingredients and put into a blender so as to make a smooth sauce. Store in the refrigerator in a bottle with a tightly fitting screw top.

Charquican (Indian Vegetable Stew)

SERVES SIX

6 potatoes, peeled and cut up	250 g minced beef
1 carrot, peeled and sliced	1 tablespoon chopped parsley
½ kg pumpkin, peeled and cut up	1 teaspoon dry ground origanum
250 g green beans, chopped	and cumin
250 g garden peas, shelled	200 g fresh corn kernels cut from
1 large tablespoon butter or 3	2 large ears of corn or defrosted
tablespoons olive oil	and chopped
½ onion, finely chopped	Salt and pepper
1 clove garlic, chopped	
1 teaspoon ají de color (see above)	

Boil the potatoes in 6 dl of salted water, together with the carrot, pumpkin, green beans and peas.

Fry the onion in the oil or butter. Add the *ají de color*, minced meat, parsley, origanum and cumin, and leave for a few minutes to incorporate.

Drain the vegetables and reserve the stock. Add the contents of the frying pan and the sweetcorn, together with 450 ml of the vegetable stock. Mix well together, season to taste and cook gently for 15 minutes more. Accompany, if desired, with pickled onions.

Chupe de Mariscos (Shellfish Stew)

SERVES SIX

6 fresh locos (or abalone from a can)
 or 12 fresh sea scallops
3 dl milk
500 g prawns, boiled and peeled or
 defrosted
250 g firm white fish
85 g butter
Bouquet garni
85 g fresh breadcrumbs soaked in
 milk
1 onion, chopped and sautéed

Salt and pepper
Dash of ají de color or ½
 teaspoon each of powdered
 cayenne pepper and hot paprika
3 hard-boiled eggs, sliced
100 g grated cheddar cheese
Dry breadcrumbs
Ground parsley
1 fresh pepper, cooked and cut into
 strips

If using canned abalone, strain the fish and cut it into 6 slices. Alternatively, simmer the scallops in the milk, reserving the fish and milk separately.

Simmer the white fish with the *bouquet garni* for 10 minutes. Reserve the stock and remove the bones and skin of the fish.

Melt the butter in a frying pan and sauté the *locos* or scallops, the prawns and white fish. Add the fresh breadcrumbs, the sautéed onion, salt, pepper and *ají de color*. Now arrange the fish in an oven-proof dish in layers, adding half of the hard-boiled eggs and grated cheese, the milk and fish stock. Cover with dry breadcrumbs and cook in a medium oven (180°C, 350°F, or Gas Mark 4) for ½ hour. Garnish with parsley, strips of pepper and the remainder of the hard-boiled egg before serving.

Empanadas de Horno (Savoury Pasties)

TO MAKE EIGHTEEN

PASTRY

1 kg sieved flour
200 g butter
150 ml white wine
2 egg yolks
325 ml brine (made with 1
 level tablespoon salt)
1 egg, for brushing

FILLING

6 medium onions, finely chopped
6 tablespoons olive oil
3 teaspoons ají de color (see p.155)
1 teaspoon dry origanum
Pepper to taste
Chillis to taste
½ kg minced beef
1 tablespoon flour
250 g stoned olives
2 or 3 hard-boiled eggs, sliced

Sauté the onion in hot olive oil with the *ají de color*, origanum, pepper and chillis. Add the minced meat and leave on a low fire until the onion is cooked and for a few minutes more until all is well blended. Sprinkle in the flour, mix well and season to taste. The mixture should be fairly juicy. Leave to cool.

Sieve the flour on to a slab and pour the hot melted butter into it. Knead with the hands until free of lumps. Now add the wine and egg-yolks, thoroughly incorporating them, then pour in the hot brine and knead well until the dough is smooth and firm. Cover, so that it does not get cold, and rest for 10 to 15 minutes.

Take amounts of dough rather smaller than a tennis ball, leaving the rest of the dough covered. Knead them well, then roll them out in the form of discs about 18 to 20 cm diameter and 2 to 3 mm thick.

In the centre of each, put 2 tablespoons of the filling, one olive and one slice of hard-boiled egg. Seal the edges of the pasties, moistening them with water, then trim them and go over them with a pastry wheel and make three folds. The edges must be wet so that they stick.

Finally, brush the pasties with beaten egg, place them on a baking sheet and bake in a moderate oven (180°C, 350°F or Gas No. 4) for 30 to 40 minutes.

Humitas (Indian Vegetable Rolls)

SERVES SIX

1 onion, finely chopped
100 g butter
1 teaspoon ají de color *(see p.155)*
700 g fresh corn kernels from 7 large
ears

1 sprig basil
Salt, pepper and chilli or sugar to
taste

Carefully strip the husks from the ears, soak the largest in hot water for 30 minutes, press on a cloth to remove excess water and reserve for wrapping up the filling.

Sauté the onion in the hot, melted butter with the *ají de color*. Put the corn kernels and basil into a blender with a little milk so as to make a smooth paste. Mix this with the onion and season to taste with salt, pepper, and chilli or sugar. The mixture should be smooth, but not too runny to wrap with the husks; if it is too thick or dry, add a little more milk.

Distribute the filling between the husks – 2 or more will be needed for each packet – rolling them up and securing them with thread or strips of husk. Boil in plenty of water for 30 to 40 minutes.

Pastel de Choclo (Sweetcorn Pie)

SERVES SIX TO EIGHT

½ kg fresh corn kernels cut from
   5 large ears or defrosted and
   chopped
3 dl milk
3 tablespoons raisins
120 g butter or margarine
1 large onion, chopped fine

½ kg best minced beef
½ breast chicken, fried in olive oil
   and cut into strips
12 olives, stoned
1 egg
2 hard-boiled eggs, sliced
2 tablespoons granulated sugar

Put the corn kernels into a blender with a little milk, so as to obtain a thick cream. Soak the raisins in 6 tablespoons of hot water for 15 minutes. Drain and reserve.

Melt one-third of the butter in a frying pan and cook the creamed corn kernels for about 10 minutes. Reserve.

Melt a little more butter in another pan, sauté the onion until transparent, then add the minced beef and continue cooking for another 15 minutes. Add the olives and raisins. Remove from the fire and add the stiffly beaten egg white and the yolk, mixing well.

Smear a round-oven dish with butter and empty into it the beef mixture. Top with a layer of hard-boiled egg, a second of fried chicken, and cover with the cooked cream of sweetcorn. Sprinkle with the sugar and cook in a medium oven (180°c, 350°c or Gas Mark 4) for 30 minutes, then increase the heat to 233°c, 450°f or Gas Mark 8 and cook for 10 minutes more until the top is golden brown.

Serve hot and straight from the oven dish.

Porotos Granados Con Pirco (Indian Bean Stew)

SERVES SIX

1 kg fresh cranberry beans or
   ½ kg dried haricot beans
1 ½ litres chicken stock
2 or 3 leaves of basil
½ kg pumpkin, peeled and cut up
2 tablespoons olive oil
1 onion, finely chopped
1 level teaspoon ají de color (see
   p.155)

1 teaspoon finely chopped parsley
1 teaspoon dry origanum
200 g fresh corn kernels from
   2 large ears or defrosted and
   chopped
Salt and pepper

If fresh cranberry beans are not available, use haricot beans, covering them with boiling water until they double in volume (around 3 hours) and then boiling them for about 1 ½ to 2 hours.

Shell the cranberry beans and boil them for 45 minutes in the chicken stock until tender. When half-cooked, add the pumpkin and leave on a low fire until tender.

Sauté the onion in hot olive oil with the *ají de color*, parsley and origanum and add to the saucepan. Add the corn kernels, salt and pepper to taste, and cook on a low fire for another 15 minutes.

Serve in hot soup plates with a little *Pebre* (hot pepper sauce).

To make Pebre

1 medium onion, finely chopped
1 clove garlic, chopped
3 tablespoons fresh coriander
2 tablespoons chopped parsley
2 green peppers, deseeded and
   finely chopped

3 tablespoons olive oil
2 tablespoons fresh lemon juice
Salt to taste

Stir together all the ingredients in a bowl and leave for about 1 hour before using.

Dulce de Membrillo Pasado (Quince Paste)

This may be eaten as a sweet; alternatively, it goes very well with cheese.

Peel and quarter the quinces, then put them into a copper pan with a few tablespoonfuls of water, being careful to retain some of the pips, and cook on the stove over a gentle fire until soft. Rub the quinces through a sieve and return the purée to the pan, together with the liquid in which they have been cooked. Add granulated sugar equal in weight to the pulp, mix and boil, stirring all the time, until a drop removed with skimmer on to a plate remains in a blob without spreading out.

Now boil the contents of the pan until thick. If desired, a small amount of breadcrumbs may be added to obtain a firmer consistency. Transfer to a shallow baking tin and dry in a warm oven. Allow the paste to cool and cut into squares or strips.

Hojuelas

These crisp golden fritters are a favourite dessert. They are served with hot golden syrup.

6 egg yolks
1 teaspoon vinegar
Sieved flour

Butter or cooking fat for frying
Icing sugar

Beat the egg yolks with the vinegar until foamy. Add enough flour to make a smooth dough which does not stick to the fingers. Knead well, then roll out into a thin sheet and cut into long strips. Melt the butter or cooking fat and fry the *hojuelas* rapidly until light golden. Place them on a kitchen paper, taking care not to break them, so as to absorb excess fat. Sprinkle them with icing sugar and serve with hot golden syrup on the side.

Papayas en Almibar (Papayas in Syrup)

SERVES FOUR TO EIGHT

Papayas must be cooked before being eaten.

1 kg papayas
1 kg granulated sugar

1 vanilla pod or cinnamon stick

Always choose hard papayas, as they are easier to peel. Use a very sharp knife, and having peeled them, make a slit in the side and remove the pips with a teaspoon.

Now place them in a bowl and blanch for 5 minutes, reserving the water. Remove to a plate, draining well and washing out the cavities left by the pips. Place the fruit, free of water, in the scales and measure out the same weight of sugar. Put the sugar into a large saucepan, then some of the reserved water, so that it is 2 cm higher than the sugar. Add the vanilla pod or cinnamon stick and heat on a medium fire until the liquid begins to thicken. Add the papayas and continue heating until they are transparent, from time to time turning them carefully so as not to break the fruit and spooning the syrup on top.

Allow to cool, then transfer to a serving dish and serve cold with cream.

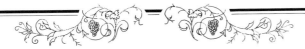

The New Wine Law

Ley que fija normas sobre producción, elaboración y comercialización de alcoholes etilicos, bebidas alcoholicas y vinagres

This law, drawn up in consultation with the wine industry, establishes a code of practice for all connected with the production of wines and alcoholic beverages, replacing Libro I of Law No. 17,105, Since it runs to 67 clauses, only a summary of the most important provisions is given.

General Provisions

After distinguishing between the products of fermentation and distillation, the preamble charges the appropriate authorities to implement the provisions of the law and more specifically:

To draw up a register of vineyards, wineries and bottlers and their processing equipment.

To take steps for the control of production, bottling, sales, importation and exportation, as laid down by the law.

To determine methods of analysis, ensuring the purity and potability of the beverages covered by the law.

To sanction laboratories to carry out these analyses.

Only the raw materials authorized by the law may be used in making alcoholic drinks. The use of other materials or subsequent adulteration is strictly prohibited.

The end products covered by the law are defined as:

Alcohols
Liquors, beverages made by fermentation, and vinegars
Chichas (*see p.55*)

Government inspectors are entitled to requisition samples at any stage in the production, distribution and commercialization of alcoholic beverages. If the producer does not agree with the results of their analysis, steps are laid down for further analyses.

Most importantly (and for the first time), growers are required to give advance notice in writing of the planting of new vines or the rooting up of vineyards, specifying the vine varieties involved.

Titulo II

This deals with beverages elaborated with ethyl alcohol, the sole type which may be used, covering brandy, whisky, gin, vodka, etc. Only alcohol containing less than a scheduled amount of impurities may be employed.

Titulo III

Titulo III is devoted to fermented beverages, in particular wine and beer.

Wine may be made only by the fermentation of fresh or sunned grapes of the species *Vitis vinifera*. The product of the alcoholic fermentation of grapes not belonging to the species *Vitis vinifera* may not be named wine, nor may it be sold under the name reserved in present law for any other alcoholic beverage. The label or container must indicate that it is an alcoholic product made from hybrid grapes.

In the vinification and elaboration of wines, it is forbidden to add alcohol, sugar in any form, or artificial sweetening agents. It is also forbidden to mix with wine any alcohol product made from hybrid grapes. Products obtained by vinification may be sweetened only with sugar proceeding from the grapes.

The very presence in a winery of sugar, glucose, artificial sweeteners or alcoholic products proceeding from hybrid vines, will be taken as evidence that such products have been used in making the wine in contravention of the provisions of the law.

Titulo IV

This relates to the manufacture of vinegar.

Titulo V

The fifth section enables the President of the Republic, through the Ministry of Agriculture, to establish demarcated regions and *denominaciones de origen* (*appellations d'origine*) for wines and distillates in parts of the country where they are justified by climate, soil, vine varieties, and viticultural and oenological practices.

For the present, the law details only three such *denominaciones de origen*:

a) Pisco: a *denominación* reserved for the brandy produced and elaborated in Regions III and IV, made by the distillation of wine proceeding from the grapes authorized in the region.

b) Pajarete: a *denominación* applying to the fortified wine produced and bottled in Regions III and IV and proceeding from the approved grape varieties.

c) Vino Asoleado: a *denominación* reserved for the fortified wine produced and bottled in the unirrigated area between the River Mataquito in the north and the River Bío-Bío in the south, made from the grapes cultivated in the area.

It is emphasized that the presence in an establishment making pisco of any of the products derived from hybrid vines will render it liable to prosecution.

Titulo VI

This covers in some detail the sale of alcoholic beverages.

They may not be sold to the consumer in containers holding more than five litres, and the label must incorporate the following minimum information:

Name and address of the bottler
Name or nature of the contents
Alcohol content
Volume of the contents

Foreign imports must be labelled with the country of origin and the name and address of the importer and distributor.

Wine sold in bottles must contain not less than 11.5 per cent of alcohol by volume and not more than 1.5 g/litre of volatile acid, except for fortified wines, for which the minimum alcohol content is 14 per cent by volume. Wines from certain southerly areas affected by unfavourable climatic conditions may by special decree be sold with only 10.5 per cent by volume of alcohol.

Imported products must conform with the minimum requirements for domestic, with which they may not be blended, and must be submitted for analysis before being sold.

Titulos VII and VIII
Disregard of any of the provisions of the law is punishable by fines, sequestration of merchandise or by enforced closure of the offending establishment. This section contains a detailed schedule of penalties appropriate to different infractions of the code.

Pencil drawing of the house of the Ezzaguirra family of Los Vascos

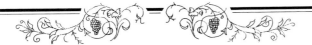

APPENDIX TWO

Exports of Chilean Wine 1986

	Bottled (cases)	*Bulk* (litres)
Andorra	2,150	—
Australia	357	—
Belgium	4,199	103,700
Bolivia	53,003	—
Brazil	203,107	—
Canada	36,399	467,500
Colombia	139,234	—
Costa Rica	15,126	—
Denmark	373	—
Dominican Republic	11,183	—
Dutch Antilles	1,030	—
Ecuador	44,047	—
El Salvador	6,140	—
France	5,060	—
Guatemala	6,981	—
Haiti	3,654	—
Holland	225	—
Honduras	1,370	—
Japan	9,384	1,021,943
Mexico	364	—
New Zealand	650	—
Panama	25,648	—
Paraguay	143,595	—
Peru	7,789	—

	Bottled (cases)	Bulk (litres)
Puerto Rico	2,631	—
South Africa	435	—
Spain	9,030	—
Sweden	1,007	—
Switzerland	220	180,449
Tahiti	2,055	75,914
UK	16,064	—
Uruguay	4,463	—
USA	209,160	61,000
Venezuela	63,819	—
West Germany	9,655	19,050
TOTALS	1,039,607	1,929,556

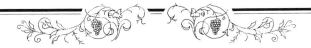

Glossary of Wine-terms used in Chile

Note: Terms appearing on labels are separately listed on *p.70*

AGUARDIENTE	Grape spirit.
ALEMBIQUE	A pot still for distilling brandy.
ARROPE	A syrup made by evaporating down must.
BARRICA	A small cask for maturing wine.
BODEGA	An establishment for making wine.
BOMBA	A pump.
BRAZO	One of the main branches of a vine.
CARAMAYOLA	A flagon similar in shape to the German *bocksbeutel.*
CATADOR	A wine-taster.
CEPA	A wine stock.
CEPAJE	*Encépagement* — the blend of grape varieties used in making a wine.
CHICHA	Young, partially fermented wine.
COOPERATIVA	A cooperative winery.
COSECHA	Harvest, vintage.
COSECHERO	Owner of a vineyard, often used of the small independent producers.
CUBA	A fermentation vat.
DEGUSTACIÓN	Tasting.

DENOMINACIÓN DE ORIGEN	The demarcation of a wine or spirit from an officially recognized region, corresponding to the French *Appellation d'Origine.*
ELABORACIÓN	The making and further treatment of wine.
EN BLANCO	A term used of the fermentation of wine without the skins or pips.
ENOLOGÍA	The science of wine-making.
ENOLÓGICO	An oenologist.
ETIQUETA	A label. For a list of terms commonly used on labels, *see p.70.*
EXPORTACIÓN	Export.
EXPORTADOR	Exporter, shipper.
FUDRE	A large wooden barrel for maturing wine.
GERENTE	The manager of a winery.
GRANEL, A	In bulk.
GRANO	The berry of the grape.
HECTAREA (HA)	A hectare of 2,471 acres.
HECTOLITRO (HL)	A hectolitre of 22 gallons.
HOLLEJO	A grape skin.
GRADO	Degree of alcohol; 13° means 13 per cent by volume.
INGENIERO AGRONOMO	An agronomist.
INJERTO	A graft.
LICOR	Liqueur, spirit.
LITRO	A litre of 1.76 pints.
LEVADURA	A yeast or ferment.
MISTELA	A sweet must in which fermentation has been arrested by the addition of alcohol.
MOSTO	Must, the juice extracted from the grapes prior to fermentation.
ORUJO	The skins and pips of the grapes removed before or after fermentation.
PAJERETE	A sweet, fortified wine.
PIPA	A pip.
PIPEÑO	Unfiltered wine containing the by-products of fermentation.
PISCO	The colourless brandy typical of Chile.
PODA	Pruning.
PORTAINJERTO	The resistant stock used when wines are grafted.
PRENSA	A wine-press.

RACIMO	A bunch of grapes.
RASPÓN	A stalk.
RAULÍ	The South American beech (*Nothofagus procera*), of which the wood is much used for making barrels and vats.
REGLAMENTO	The rules detailing the making of wines or spirits covered by a *denominación de origen*.
RIEGO	Irrigation.
ROBLE	Oak.
SARMIENTO	A wine shoot.
SOCIO	A partner in a cooperative winery.
TOLVA	An Archimedean screw used for transferring the fruit to the crusher.
TREN	A bottling line.
UVA	A grape.
VENDIMIA	The wine harvest.
VID	A vine.
VIÑA	1. a vineyard, 2. a wine company, e.g. Viña Undurraga.
VIÑEDO	A vineyard.
VINICULTURA	The science and practice of wine-making.
VINO	Wine (*see also p.70*).
VINO ASOLEADO	Wine made from sunned grapes.
VINO DEL AÑO	Wine from the last harvest.
VITICULTOR	A wine-grower.
VITICULTURA	The cultivation of vines for wine-making.
ZONA DE SECANO	An unirrigated wine area.

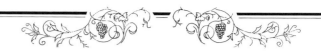

Bibliography

Alavarado Moore, Rodrigo, *Chile, Tierra del Vino*, 2nd ed., Santiago, 1985. *Los motivos del vino* (collected articles), privately printed, 1984.

Byron, John, *The Narrative of the Honourable John Byron*, London, 1768.

Carola cocina, Editorial Antarctica SA, Santiago, n.d.

Chile, An Exporting Country for Fruit and Vegetables, Basel (International Fruit World), n.d.

Clissold, Stephen, *Bernardo O'Higgins and the Independence of Chile*, London, 1968.

Cooperativa Agrícola Pisquera Elqui Ltda, *El valle donde los hombres transforman el sol en Pisco*, Vicuña, n.d.

Dundonald, Thomas Cochrane, Tenth Earl of, *Narrative of Services in the Liberation of Chili, Peru and Brazil*, London, 1859.

Guía Gourmet, Commercial ITV Ltda, Santiago, 1982.

Herring, Hubert, *A History of Latin America*, 3rd ed., London, 1968.

Illustrated London News, *The Vintage at Macul,Chile*, 5 Oct., 1889.

INIA (Instituto de Investigaciones Agropecuarias), *Posibilidades de la vitivinicultura del area de Cauquenes, VII Region del Maule*, Cauquenes, 1980.

Johnson, Hugh, *World Atlas of Wine*, new ed., London, 1985. *Wine Companion*, London, 1984.

La sabrosa geografía de Chile, Centro Nestlé de Información al Consumidor, Santiago, n.d.

Lambert Ortiz, Elizabeth, *The Book of Latin American Cookery*, London, 1984.

Leonard, Jonathon Norton, and the Editors of Time-Life Books, *Latin American Cooking*, Time Inc., 1970.

Ministerio de Hacienda, *Proyecto de ley que fija normas sobre producción, elaboración y comercializición de alcoholes etílicos, bebidas alcoholicas y vinagres*. Deroga Libro I de la Ley No. 17,105.

Ossandon Guzman, Carlos and Mujica Gutierrez, Bernadita, *Guía de Santiago*, 7th ed., Santiago, 1983.

Paz Lagarrigue, María, *Recetas de las Rengifo*, 16th ed., Santiago, 1983.

Pro-Chile (Chilean Traditional Wine Exporter Committee), *official catalogue*, Santiago, n.d.

Read, Jan, *Lord Cochrane*, Caracas (Plata Press), 1977. *The New Conquistadores*, London, 1980.

Rodriguez, J., Sierra, C. and Araos, F., *Niveles de fertilidad en los suelos de la Zona Centro Norte*, in *Ciencia e investigación agraria*, No. 4.

Rovira Pinto, Adriano, *Geografía de Chile*, Tomo V, *Geografía de los suelos*, Santiago (Instituto Geográfico Militar), 1984.

Stevens, David, *The Wines of South America*, in *André Simon's Wines of the World*, 2nd ed., London, 1981.

The South American Handbook, Bath (Trade & Travel Publications Ltd.), 1986.

Torres, Miguel A., *Viñas y vinos de Chile*, in *Encuentros con el vino*, No. 1, 1985.

Undurraga Vicuña, Francisco Ramón, *Recuerdos de ochenta años*, Santiago, n.d.

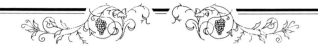

Picture Acknowledgements

All the illustrations are the author's with the exception of the following: pages 30–3, *Illustrated London News*, 5 Oct. 1889 (The Vintage in Chile: sketches by our special artist, Mr Melton Prior); page 89, Viña Concha y Toro, S.A. The source for the map on page 43 comes from Rodrigo Alvarez Moore's *Chile Tierra del Vino* and the maps on pages 43 and 45 have been redrawn from sources issued by the Instituto Geografico Militar.

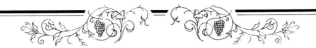

Index

Page numbers in italics refer to illustrations

ESTATE BOTTLED

Monte Cañeten

1984

COLCHAGUA
SAUVIGNON
BLANC

Grown, Produced and Bottled by
Viña Los Vascos, Peralillo, Chile.
Imported by Wines of the World, Inc.
New York, NY, U.S.A.
PRODUCT OF CHILE
Alcohol 12.4% by Volume · Contents 750ml.

Errazuriz Panquehue M.R.

CORTON
GRAN VINO M.R.

Vino Elaborado y Embotellado por Viña Errázuriz-Panquehue Ltda.
Panquehue, San Felipe - CHILE

1982
LOS VASCO

CABERNET SAUV
Peralillo, Colchag

Vino Fino Producido y E
en Origen por Viña Lo
PRODUCT OF C
Propietarios
Jorge Eyzaguirre   María I.

EMBOTELLADO EN ORIGEN

Castillo de Molina
CABERNET SAUVIGNON
VINTAGE 1978

VIÑA SAN PEDRO
DESDE 1865

CONTENTS 750 ML ALCOHOL 12% BY VOL

20.000
BOTELLAS
SAN PEDRO

PRODUCED & BOTT

IMPORTE
OF

WINES CORP
A. 33126

FOUNDED IN 1880

Santa Rita
MAIPO VALLEY CHILE

1986
SAUVIGNON BLANC
ESTATE BOTTLED

EXPORT WINE PRODUCED AND BOTTLED BY VIÑA SANTA RITA LTDA.
BY VOL. 12%

EXPOSICION

Piña Espumante

Vino Suave Gasificado. Envasado en Origen por C.A. Vitivinícola de Talca Ltda. Avda. San Miguel 2631 - Talca - Región del Maule.
Grado mínimo 90 G.L. - Producto Chileno - Contenido 750 c.c.

Licores

Campana

CONTENIDO 750 c.c.   PROD
LA SERENA IV REGION   GRADO A
ELABORADO POR COOP. AGRICOL
PISQUERO DE ELQUI LTD

DAMASC

zuriz Panq

DOÑA LEON
ANTIGUA RESERVA

Vino Elaborado y Embotellado por Viña Errázuriz
Panquehue..San Felipe - CHILE

Pisco
capel
selección 30°

PRODUCIDO Y EMBOTELLADO EN EL VALLE DE ELQUI (VICUNAL PROVINCIA DE ELQUI CHILE
POR COOPERATIVA AGRICOLA PISQUERA ELQUI LTDA. CAMINO A PERALILLO S/N
CONTENIDO 585 C.C.

CABERNET SAUVIGNON

Santa Emiliana
1982
CONCHA y TORO

VINOS EXPOSICION

Conde del Maule

Envasado en Origen por C. A. Vitivinícola de Talca Ltda.
Avda. San Miguel 2631 — Talca
REGION DEL MAULE
Grado Mínimo 11,7 G.L. Producto Chileno Contenido 700 c.c.

VIÑA MAI
Importado por Importaciones Colombia Ltda.
Registro Minsalud N.º L 000240

Chilean
Burgundy

Grado Alcoholico 12° G.L.
Contenido neto 0,70 L
PRODUCTO CHILENO

Producido
Viña Maipo

Vino Chileno de Exportación